At HOME with ART

At HOME
with ART

How

ART LOVERS

Live with

and Care for Their

COLLECTIONS

ESTELLE ELLIS   CAROLINE SEEBOHM   CHRISTOPHER SIMON SYKES

 Thames & Hudson

To my daughter, Nora,

and to Harriet and Miki

for their friendship and gentle counsel.

To my son, Ellis,

for sharing the pleasure of art at home.

—E.E.

For Morley and Renee, my favourite artists.

—C.S.

For my brothers and sisters.

—C.S.S.

HALF TITLE

Cross Aweigh *(1967) by Alfonso Ossorio. Collection of Ted Dragon.*

FRONTISPIECE

A world of art meets on a mantel in the Dunlops' London flat:
a painting by Scottish colourist Francis B. Cadell, torso by
British sculptor Stephen Cox, Mughal miniature, South Indian
mounted figure, two Congolese sculptures.

CHAPTER OPENERS

Details of paintings (various) by Max Gimblett.

Permissions are on page 247.

First published in the United Kingdom in 1999 by Thames & Hudson Ltd,
181A High Holborn, London WC1V 7QX

British Library Cataloguing-in-Publication Data
A catalogue record for this book is available from the British Library

ISBN 0-500-01967-3

Printed in China

ACKNOWLEDGMENTS

There would be no book without the generosity of the art-lovers who welcomed us into their homes to photograph their treasures. Their patience and personal stories have been invaluable to us.

We would also like to thank those many others who talked to us about their experiences of living with art, including: George and Meda Abrams, John Bryant and Patricia Bauman, Linda Connor, Charles Cowles, Georges and Lois de Menil, Bunny Dell, Charles and Valerie Diker, Ted Dragon, Frank Faulkner, Cornelia Foss, Alvin Friedmankien, Joellen Hall, Ann Hatch, Richard Hennessy, Timothy Greenfield-Sanders, Gerald and Jane Katcher, Betty Klausner, Phyllis Kluger, Jeffrey and Dina Knapp, Pierre and Rose Levai, Peter Menendez, Henry and Maria Livingston, Joel and Sherry Mallin, Sam and Rosetta Miller, Charlotte Parks, Rudolph Railey and the late Suzanne Railey, Robert Rosenblum, Michael Rosenfeld and Halley Harrisburg, Thomas and Bonnie Rosse, Frederic and Jean Sharf, Mr. and Mrs. Gursharan Sidhu, Philip M. Smith, Don and Taki Wise.

We are greatly indebted to the many experts and friends who led us to art-filled homes, offered hospitality, and whose knowledge of art gave authority to the project, including: Peter Barna, Flora and Sydney Biddle, Leslie Chang, Jim and Morley Clark, Marc Cohen, Jack Cowart, Madison Cox, Miki Denhof, Michele Oka Doner, Massumeh Farhad, Ruth Fine, Charlotte Gere, Max Gimblett, Harriet Wilinsky Goodman, Cheryl Haines, Mark Hampton, Katherine Hinds, David Kermani, Jack Lenor Larsen, Rex Lau, Walter Lippincott, Sonia Lopez, Stanley Marcus, Paula Matisse, Katherine Miller, Richard Minsky, Alexandra Munroe, Mary Jane Pool, Lois Prievant, Toby Carr Rafelson, Allen Rosenbaum, Robert Rosenkranz, Ruth and Marvin Sackner, Edwina Sandys and Richard Kaplan, Claire and Maurice Segal, Mike Solomon, Allan Stone, Jane Stubbs, John Stubbs, Patricia Sullivan, Patricia Tang, Joan Vass, Jonathan Waxman, William Weber, Ann Yonemura, Deborah Ziska.

Appreciation is also expressed for the donation of supplementary art, photography, and poetry: Susan Baran, Katherine Gerlough at The Frick Collection, Maureen O'Hara, Edda Renouf, Eugene Thaw, Dorothy and Herbert Vogel, Christopher Woodward at Sir John Soane's Museum, John Yau.

The publishing of a complex illustrated book requires diligence and expertise. We were fortunate to have on our team the discerning eye and impeccable taste of our editor, Carol Southern, who lived with the book from its birth to its maturity. Roy Finamore guided us with his sharp editorial skills and publishing know-how. Art director, Marysarah Quinn, navigated the design process with sensitivity and enthusiasm. As in *At Home with Books,* Susan Carabetta sorted through a dizzying number of images and again came up with a visually arresting design. With care and competence, Christopher Smith, Vincent La Scala, and Joan Denman shepherded the book through the production labyrinth. Commendation to Christa Bourg for her dedicated research, writing, and organizing support. We also thank our agents, Loretta Barrett and Helen Pratt, for their confidence.

In particular, we express our gratitude to artist Max Gimblett for granting us permission to use details from his evocative paintings for the chapter dividers in this book.

CONTENTS

ABOVE

Roz Jacobs's collection of antique irons, begun with Man Ray and including his Le Fer Rouge, *climb the staircase in her New York apartment.*

TOP

Undine by Boris Lovet Lorski from John Axelrod's mantel.

PARTNERS IN ART

THE WRITER'S VISION

PICTURE-PERFECT SPACES

David Hockney's portrait of Celia is hung over a window (why not, since there is no view?), in Barbara Davidson's color and light-flooded Florida living room.

The Hampstead studio—living room of British artist Derek Hill

is proof that he feels very much at home with his art.

INTRODUCTION

I n 1994, when three explorers discovered the Chauvet cave in southeast France, which contained more than three hundred paintings and engravings of bears, lions, mammoths, and rhinoceroses dating from over 30,000 years ago, the emotion that gripped them made them incapable of uttering a word. They felt "as if the tens of thousands of years that separated us from the producers of these paintings no longer existed. It seemed as if they had just created these masterpieces." These awestruck explorers were surely witnessing the dawn of art.

The presence of art in the cave sanctuaries of our earliest ancestors connects us with these artists in a way that is more moving than the mere revelation of their talent and skill. "Our humanity derives from shared experiences in the remote past," writes John D. Barrow in *The Artful Universe,* "when many of our propensities were acquired as adaptations to a universal environment." Art, then and now, reflects those distant experiences by producing images that flicker across our universal consciousness, resonating visually, emotionally, and spiritually from a common pool of experience and a need for larger meaning.

Art, along with music, literature, and science, also offers the promise that some sort of order can be created out of our chaotic world. The artist reconciles opposing forces, producing harmony out of conflict, offering us an escape from confusion. Art in this sense is a pathway to consolation and the soul's peace.

Our appreciation of the Phillips Collection in Washington, D.C., for instance, is the greater when we learn that it was inspired by the tragic loss of Duncan Phillips's father and brother. Phillips wrote:

> I TURNED TO MY LOVE OF PAINTING FOR THE WILL TO LIVE. ART OFFERS TWO GREAT GIFTS OF EMOTION—THE EMOTION OF RECOGNITION AND THE EMOTION OF ESCAPE. BOTH EMOTIONS TAKE US OUT OF THE BOUNDARIES OF SELF. . . . AT MY PERIOD OF CRISIS I WAS PROMPTED TO CREATE SOMETHING WHICH WOULD EXPRESS MY AWARENESS TO LIFE'S RETURNING JOYS AND MY POTENTIAL ESCAPE INTO THE LAND OF ARTISTS' DREAMS. I WOULD CREATE A COLLECTION OF PICTURES . . . LAYING EVERY BLOCK IN ITS PLACE WITH A VISION OF THE WHOLE EXACTLY AS THE ARTIST BUILDS HIS MONUMENT OR HIS DECORATION.

Every spectrum of the search for spiritual as well as visual gratification is reflected in *At Home with Art*. We were constantly confounded by the variety and eclecticism of the art lovers we encountered, from the almost accidental discovery by Jason Vass that political posters were more important to him than any of his other youthful interests, to the lifetime commitment of Dorothy and

Artists Gilbert & George have chosen to live in their small East London house surrounded by nineteenth-century pottery by Christopher Dresser and Sir Edmund Elton, rather than paintings.

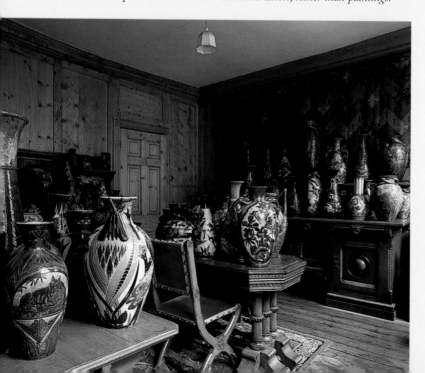

Architecture (arched window with moldings) and art (by Mark Katano) work well together in this stairwell in the Hobsons' San Francisco townhouse.

Herbert Vogel, who set aside half their income to buy conceptual art when it was considered obscure and esoteric. Some, who inherited art, developed an early awareness of its joys and the historical meaning of their legacy, and are now pondering the complexity of its passage to children and/or museums. Others, who received gifts from artist friends, create surroundings that extend the pleasure of their company. Still others simply started out with bare walls and made impulse buys that later turned into love affairs. These often included the work of young artists, who discovered they had eager patrons.

Many developed an involvement with art that has required commitment, energy, courage, vision, and a reordering of priorities. John Axelrod gave up a legal and business career to become a full-time art collector. He filled every room in his spacious floor-through apartment with an idiosyncratic mix of paintings, sculpture, furniture, and ceramics, knowing he would have little room left for entertaining and no room at all for overnight guests. Ramón and Nercys Cernuda risked controversy

Ellsworth Kelly's Diagonal with Curve VI *hovers like a bolt of blue lightning over the Katcher family (Jane, Elizabeth, Katherine, Gerald, and Margaret, in front) in their Florida living room. "When I look at it," Gerry says, "I remember what Kelly said to us about it, where we bought it, and how deeply Jane felt about it."*

and faced legal and social harassment to claim their right to live with Cuban art. Partnership in marriage produced a dynamic alliance for Agnes Gund and Daniel Shapiro; her modern masters cohabit harmoniously with his Chinese and African antiquities. Civil rights lawyer Eric Robertson turned to the art of his ancestors to satisfy his desire to give his life and work equal meaning. Mary Jane Harris fell in love at first sight with Italian baroque painting and has lived with it happily ever after. Her romantic attachment reflects the feeling of Phyllis Rose, who, in her memoir, *The Year of Reading Proust,* admits that "I have reached the age when collecting is the stage on which I enact desire."

The second life that art has given so many in this book is illuminated by Edward Albee's decision to create a foundation and an artist-writer colony to support aspiring creative talent. Unabashed art lovers, our contributors derive much of their pleasure from the process of educating themselves. Over and over again, we heard, "The education of the eye is an ongoing process. You have to look, look, look, read, and experience." In several cases, spouses educated each other to respect and even grew to love each other's taste. Parents engaged their children in the experience of choosing art for their walls. In almost every room we found shelves filled with books, catalogs, and magazines on art.

As personal as the choice of art is the singular way these individuals incorporate it into their homes. The integration of art with living space is ultimately what this book is celebrating. The Key Biscayne condominium of Martin Margulies, for instance, was constructed to give his art dramatic dominance, thus furniture and color schemes are sublimated to the paintings and sculpture. In the 1832 home of Harry van Dyke, on the other hand, the art is in harmony with authentic nineteenth-century furniture and decorative objects, appropriate choices for a landmark house that overlooks the Hudson Valley. Laurence Strenger's dazzling array of prints and drawings has in effect taken over his New York apartment like an invading army. John and Frances Bowes's house in Sonoma was specifically designed to encompass the large contemporary

The entryhall of Albee's Montauk home sets the stage for the African and contemporary artworks he enjoys. Lee Krasner's painting and Diane Mayo's ceramic dominate the far wall.

Charles I made sure that Sir Anthony Van Dyck included the royal spaniels in his portrait of the king's children.

canvases they love so much. For Anjelica Huston and Robert Graham, the house came first, and their pictures happily accepted this priority.

In some cases, the art becomes almost fused with its owner in an inseparable match. King Charles I, for instance, never went anywhere without miniature copies of his dog paintings. The seventeenth-century Chinese collector Zhou Lianggong installed his collection on a houseboat that served as his floating museum. When author James Lord visited Gertrude Stein in her famous art-filled Paris apartment, he was told by Alice B. Toklas to wait in the salon until his hostess arrived. "But she was already there," James Lord wrote in his memoir, *Six Exceptional Women.* "Whether present physically or not . . . Gertrude Stein always inhabited that room as long as it contained all the possessions that so vividly, historically, and imperatively substantiated her presence. These, above all, were the pictures. Where the pictures were, Gertrude Stein was."

So many different kinds of art, so many different ways of living with it. "Art has a chameleon quality," collector Jane Katcher said. "Where you see it changes how you see it." This is especially evident when the collector lives

in more than one place. Eugene Thaw explains that the old master drawings so prized by him and his wife Clare are very much at home in their softly lit European-style town house in New York, while their Native American art is well suited to their sun-filled Santa Fe retreat. "You see art differently," he said, "when you look out over skyscrapers, a mountain, or water."

How we wish to live with our art varies as much as our personal relationships. What is clear from the people who described their feelings to us in *At Home with Art* is that they all delight in the art they "possess or are possessed by," either making over their homes to its service or integrating it in such a way that life and art are one.

In the house of the late Christopher Isherwood and Don Bachardy, the many artworks are like the voices of all their friends.

5

ONE VISION

for Georgia O'Keeffe

SUSAN BARAN

What need have I of color except that which clings

to the blue sky or streaked clay of the desert?

I hoard the finest oils in tubes, mix and re-mix

to capture the energy of this planet,

the light that dances and darts from each object.

I want the form of tears, not their melancholy.

The earth is constant.

We crave the color that surrounds us, steal the last,

pink drop of sunset for a scarf to wrap our throat,

wear a skirt of plum that hugs pale hips.

Clothed in radiance and desire we pluck

the sacred day. I want none of this—

I am content in black and white,

all absence, all presence.

Only the joy of canvas

helps me see a little clearer

each time I paint, that others

may know on dove gray walls in a city

shaded by towers, obscured by the mist

of a million breaths, the stars that shine above the desert.

My pictures exist only for a brief moment

in this world, then they dry and bleach

like the bones whose scattered figures

haunt these sands, and when I too

have turned to bone, form will join form

in the order of this universe.

I will be that which I have struggled

to know through my fingertips, to see—

smooth and polished into final form

like the black river rock that rests

on a white shelf above my bed,

I shall be alone and pure.

The Passionate Collector

LAURENCE STRENGER

THE SECRET IS TO BE FOCUSED.

I don't recommend such crowding," Laurence Strenger observes, critically surveying the packed walls of his New York apartment. "But . . ." He shrugs. The profile of the ardent collector usually includes the words "addictive," "tireless," and "ambitious" and "a master of detail." Laurence Strenger fits the profile. Over thirty years he has energetically and painstakingly put together a huge collection of eighteenth- and nineteenth-century English drawings, paintings, furniture, and porcelains, accumulating "to a level of financial strain." He owns perhaps 1,200 paintings, prints, drawings, and textiles, about 300 of which hang in the New York apartment at any one time. "If I want to expand any more, I'll probably have to move," he concedes.

Such a personality, one suspects, is born, not made. As a boy, Strenger collected comic books. "My mother threw them out when I went to college," he says, still visibly annoyed. He also acquired floor plans of buildings. "I would ask developers for their blueprints." This is the fascination of the scholar for a challenging subject, the

seed passion of the collector. "I get interested in a subject and then explore it," he says.

Most summers he and his family spent time in England, at Glassenbury Park in Kent, and there he began to hone his interest in fine art. He made his first purchase in Rome in 1963 when he bought a seventeenth-century view of the Santa Maria Salute in Venice, a city that interested him at the time. He continued to enjoy landscapes, but after purchasing some Whistler drawings, he began to specialize in English works with historical, topographical, and ornithological subjects. He read books, attended exhibitions, developed relationships with dealers, kept up with the market, took an apartment in London, and became a fixture at the annual Grosvenor House art and antique show.

Meanwhile, he moved into the investment business, which called him back permanently to the United States. Twelve years ago he found an apartment in New York which he felt could accommodate his ever-increasing collection of pictures and objects. Although basically a pied-à-terre (he spends most of his working life in California in a house equally crammed with art), the New York apartment has a tremendous amount of wall space, plus only one exposure facing west. In fact the light is so strong that to protect the delicate drawings he has them framed under treated glass. He has also installed blinds that are drawn during the afternoon.

OPPOSITE

The narrow corridor in Laurence Strenger's apartment is ceiling-to-floor art. On the left is a part of his ornithological collection. At the end, a grandfather clock surrounded by prints and textiles pulls the whole display together.

The apartment, decorated with the help of Marilyn Meyerson, is now floor-to-ceiling pictures, fine English furniture, and antique porcelain, all arranged with meticulous attention to detail. The pictures are lit with halogen track lighting, which Strenger "fools around with" all the time. Yet although the place is so crowded, there is little feeling of claustrophobia. Why? Perhaps it is because there is a soothing symmetry to the placement of the pictures—generally a big picture in the middle, smaller ones around it. The frames of the pictures are also soothing, being mostly of the period, unpretentious, with simple moldings, usually plain gold. Most walls are devoted to a particular subject—important English works over the sofa in the living room, landscapes in the library, Chinese prints in the

ABOVE

ABOVE

In the bedroom, nineteenth-century engravings of people and animals are arrayed in simple gold frames of the period against a William Morris willow pattern wallcovering.

LEFT

Laurence Strenger reads beneath his eighteenth- and nineteenth-century art. The arrangement over the sofa is typical Strenger—several large pictures in the center anchoring the rest.

dining room, ornithology in the hall corridor, and so forth—thus giving coherence to the visual impact.

"I would like to have less clutter," Strenger says. "Things suffer from this arrangement. They are not optimally shown this way." But can a collector change his spots? Evidently not. To the untutored eye, there seems not one space left in the apartment to hang further acquisitions. Strenger, however, has other ideas. He indicates a minuscule opening on the hall wall. "There's some room there," he declares with a glint in his eye. He also points out three views of Chatsworth hanging over a door to the bedroom. "I could put something else there. Those prints are not important." In fact, he seems to derive pleasure from the creative challenge of finding more space. "This is my maxi-stack," he says proudly, pointing to a door frame, around which every inch is covered.

Strenger is increasingly drawn to textiles, which are even more difficult to display than drawings. Textiles are tricky to frame, and their fragility requires light-diffusing blinds to protect them. But nothing stops the acquisitive personality. Not space, not time, not the frailty of the art. "I would still buy more," he says. "The secret is to be focused. And as you see, my focus changes." Then he adds, with a resigned smile, "I suppose it never ends."

MARTIN Z. MARGULIES

WITHOUT ART, I COULD LIVE IN A TWO-BEDROOM APARTMENT, BUT BECAUSE I CAN'T LIVE WITHOUT ART, I NEED SPACE.

There is something unsettling about walking through the front door of Martin Margulies's apartment in Coconut Grove, Florida, and seeing a housekeeper standing motionless with her trolley of cleaning supplies. Duane Hanson's *Cleaning Woman "Queenie,"* made out of painted polyvinyl, is so hyperreal that window cleaners on a scaffold outside Margulies's penthouse window reported her "asleep on the job."

Queenie is one of several "petrified figures" that people Margulies's home and keep him company. Three of George Segal's cast of characters have a strong presence in the living room, seated in what appears as theatrical sets—a subway car, a bar window, and a park bench. This is the room where Martin, a builder-developer, tells you he is most comfortable working. Books, documents, and files are piled up on the deeply upholstered couch and chairs that bracket a coffee table covered with blueprints. "Art is so much a part of my life," he says, "I don't want to be separated from it."

Margulies's furniture is as unobtrusive as the art is dramatic. He has a strong taste for art with nerve, power, and energy. "I love beauty. I love excitement, and I think the art I live with makes these kinds of statements," he tells you, leading you to *Grand Vase,* a Miró ceramic that he first saw in the basement of Galerie Maeght in Paris in 1980. He takes another Miró, a gouache, off the wall to show you the stickers on the back that reveal it was once owned by Marcel Duchamp. "As I got more and more into the learning curve," Margulies explains, "I realized that this magnificent piece from Miró's Constellation series was a seminal artwork. It became the starting point of my collection."

Margulies finds great joy in being surrounded by art. "I know what's in my living room even when I'm lying in my bedroom," he says, "because the works of Kline, Rothko, Judd, and Marden have a presence in my vision, even though I may not see them all the time. I miss the collection when I'm away from it."

Katherine Hinds, who has worked closely with Margulies as curator of his collection for fifteen years, remembers, "I moved a minor piece around once and didn't tell him. He called me at ten-thirty at night to ask me where it was. When a piece is missing, he knows it.

OPPOSITE

In his bedroom, Margulies has hung two paintings by Motherwell, an artist he admires as much for his writing as his art, and a 1961 Frank Stella shaped canvas. John De Andrea's Blonde Woman *stands exposed, leavened by Alan Siegel chairs and Martin's children's toys.*

OVERLEAF

Modern and contemporary artworks keep Margulies company in his cavernous living room—Kline and Stella on the far wall; Miró's Grand Vase *next to a dividing wall with paintings by Marden* (left) *and Noland* (right); *in the foreground, Miró's painted bronze chair and Oldenburg's* Soft Baked Potato.

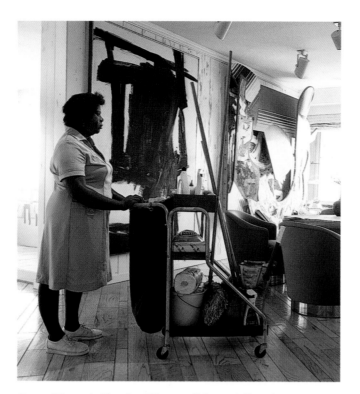

Duane Hanson's Cleaning Woman ("Queenie") *and George Segal's* Blue Girl on Black Bench *add theater and humor to the gallery-scale living room.*

16

He feels it." Hinds describes Margulies's collection as "one man's view of the history of modern sculpture and post–World War II painting. Art is a life pursuit for Marty," she says. "He bought his first piece of art, an Isamu Noguchi sculpture, in 1976 and has since built not only one of the largest private collections of Noguchi's work but one of the most comprehensive private sculpture collections in the country." Forty-five of his sculptures are on long-term loan to Florida International University.

"Marty is unrelenting," Katherine says. "He has been to every Sotheby's and Christie's auction of contemporary art and goes to every fair. He takes a trip to New York every month. He has many friends in the art world, so he's totally plugged in." Margulies looks at a work of art from many different angles and is very decisive about what he wants. "There's a thrill when you see something you really like," Margulies says. "You walk into a show, see someone's work and feel the exhilaration of the hunt. Of course, you try to contain yourself when you talk to the dealer," he says, smiling.

Martin Margulies tells you that without art, he could live anywhere. "I could live in a two-bedroom apartment," he says, "but because I can't live without art, I need space." When Margulies moved recently from Coconut Grove to the high-rise he built in Key Biscayne, his first concern was arranging twenty years of art. "We had to give it room to breathe," he says.

The logistics of moving and the orchestration of packers, handlers, drivers, and even a crane operator was daunting. Hinds, who oversaw it all, says, "Marty's new apartment was only twenty miles away, but it might as well have been two thousand. The move took a year of planning. Every piece had separate concerns. With some paintings, we worried about the change in temperature and environment. When we finally got everything in the new space, we found we could position major sculpture pieces on the terraces that face the bay on one side and the ocean on the other. We could hang the Kline next to the Twombly next to the Rothko, which we were never able to do before. We were able to create a gallery for the more conceptual artists like Bruce Nauman. Idea-oriented art doesn't mix well with the retina-oriented art of Rothko and Kline." Since Martin doesn't drink and entertains infrequently, he decided that a windowless bar area would better serve as a room for viewing light-sensitive masterworks on paper from the forties and fifties—a Pollock drip piece, a Gorky drawing, and a de Kooning painting.

Transplanting the art was both challenging and surprising. Katherine explains, "At first we thought we wanted to hang something with high impact at the far end of the apartment. But we ended up placing a subtle Morris Louis painting with an ethereal feel in this space. Just seeing it there changed our minds. We looked at each other and said, 'That's it!'"

In his new Key Biscayne apartment, Margulies built a separate wing for his children and told them they could choose any art they wanted for their rooms. His youngest son, Joseph, age seven, chose an Andy Warhol picture of Uncle Sam (he thought it was George Washington). The oldest, David, seventeen, said he only wanted Budweiser signs in his room until two of his young women friends convinced him otherwise. Sixteen-year-old Michael was undecided, but nine-year-old Elizabeth opted for wallpaper and her own drawings.

In a quiet corner of his living room is the piece Margulies says anchors his collection, Miró's 1940 gouache from his Constellation *series. Couch seating provides a direct view of a Rothko painting, a Judd minimalist sculpture over the door, and Chamberlain's crashed car parts relief.*

SARAH "SALLY" G. EPSTEIN

GOOD ART TELLS YOU SOMETHING
ABOUT YOURSELF.

I cannot imagine living with anything but Munch on my walls," Sally Epstein emphasizes. "A roomful of pink-cheeked Renoir women would make me uneasy. A roomful of abstract art would frustrate me. Introducing other artists into my home would dilute the powerful effect of what Munch called his Frieze of Life."

On hearing that Sally Epstein's five-story house in Washington, D.C., is totally devoted to the work of Edvard Munch, people ask, "How can she live with it?" But when the shades, drawn to protect the prints, are raised and you adjust to the chilly temperature, "kinder to paper than to people," you experience the pleasure Sally and her five children have found in living with Munch.

Sally attributes her affinity for this art, which has become a symbol for the angst of the twentieth century, to her career in social work. "Munch's themes relate to the anxieties my clients express—fear, loneliness, jealousy, anger, and the ambiguities of sexual love. I find his images moving, not depressing."

Sally and her former husband, Lionel Epstein, discovered Munch in the 1960s. "It was like a tidal wave swept over me," Sally remembers. Early in their marriage, Lionel

Rows of works by a single artist, Edvard Munch, are arranged up the stairwell of the Epstein home, demonstrating the progression of his art and multiplicity of his images and techniques.

bought three Munch prints for Sally. "I knew even then it was not enough to just fall in love with a piece of art," Lionel says. "Good art tells you something about yourself."

Lionel, whom Sally describes as having "the skill and taste of the hunt," coordinated his law practice travel with auctions in Europe and New York. It was a time when Munch graphics were available and the bulk of the 250 works in the Epstein family collection was purchased.

"We decided from the outset that we would build a teaching collection," Sally reveals. "To enjoy Munch you need to know about his life. That's why I've added ninety interviews with people he knew to our archive. Our family has agreed that one day it will all go to the National Gallery."

Munch's oil sketch for a portrait of his friends, the Gierloff family.

JOHN AXELROD

ART HAS FOUR DIMENSIONS, THE THREE YOU SEE AND THE FOURTH, THE STORY BEHIND IT.

John Axelrod never thought he would ever fill the Boston Back Bay condominium he moved into twenty years ago. But he has, over and over again, with an explosion of European and American Art Deco art and furniture, funky California ceramics, and more recently, African-American and South American paintings. He finally had to do away with his guest room to create space for an art library and a gallery devoted to his current passion: Argentinean and Uruguayan art. Flowing, windowless walls and 14-foot ceilings in this historic 1892 house overlooking the Charles River provide Axelrod with the ideal environment for his kaleidoscopic approach to living with art.

Described as a "man who follows his bliss," Axelrod is a lawyer who smiles when he says, "I stopped practicing because it took too much time away from my art interests." Since Axelrod arranges all the art in his home himself, he is very clear about the reasons why he groups certain artists and art periods together, as he did in the hallway where he has arranged the paintings of five social

OPPOSITE

Axelrod's passion for Art Deco furniture, furnishings, and art is concentrated in a living room that also makes room for California funk ceramics. A Robert Arneson head from his Nuclear *series is positioned by the window so that "when the sun reflects off the piece, it looks like he's on fire."*

surrealists. Or as he did in his bedroom where he has hung some of his favorite paintings, including three by artists who worked together: Paul Cadmus, Jared French, and George Tooker. Cadmus's arresting image of muscular men, *YMCA Locker Room,* hangs over Axelrod's bed, playfully positioned in counterpoint to Guy Pène du Bois's painting, *Women's Locker Room.*

"I'll sometimes get up at three o'clock in the morning and rearrange stuff," Axelrod says. "There are times when I'll put something away, but then I'll miss it and take it out again. Sometimes I want an empty look, and remembering a friend's advice—'You must give your eyes a place to rest'—I'll isolate a painting or sculpture. But then it will look strange to me, so I'll start looking for works to complement it."

When people ask Axelrod's advice about buying a particular piece, he answers: "Do you love it? Would you want to look at it first thing in the morning and the last thing at night? Everything in my house excites me because I only buy what I love. Every night before I go to sleep, I go into my gallery and look at the surrealist paintings that I bought in Argentina, six in one week and the rest over the next year. . . .

"Art has four dimensions," Axelrod tells you, "the three you see and the story behind the artwork—that is the fourth. I was visiting a friend's house in Argentina and discovered that he had several artworks from one of

Axelrod's gallery/library, with its extensive collection of books on Argentinean art, is an homage to Argentine artists from El Grupo Orion, among them a work by Ideal Sanchez and a signature piece by Luis Barragán.

the first surrealist groups in South America, El Grupo Orion. I thought they were fabulous and asked if he was willing to part with them. He agreed, explaining he was ready to sell because for years he had been unable to acquire a painting by Ideal Sanchez, whose work would complete the collection. I sent the paintings home and, later on, called Sanchez to ask him if he would do a portrait of me. We discovered we shared a love of dogs, and it prompted him to do a dream sequence of me as a young boy, romping with my dogs. After the third sitting, I asked if he had any paintings left from the Orion group. He said, 'Yes, the one I did in homage to my parents.' When I told him I'd love to have it, he hesitated at first, but then agreed. That's what I mean when I tell you there is always a story behind the art you live with."

Axelrod's compulsion to acquire art can be seen in the way he has furnished his home. "When I moved into my own place and I wanted to decorate it, I fell in love with Art Deco," he says, "and I started to educate myself. I still have the first thing I bought, a 1928 Gene Theobald tea set. I had no idea what it was, but it turned out to be a classic."

The hallway, bedroom, and living room (once the library of this grand scale house) are a testament to Axelrod's love for American Art Deco furniture. Paul Frankl cabinets, tables, and sofa give the living room its streamlined 1930s style. A circular Frankl mirror, reminiscent of the 1939 New York World's Fair perisphere, occupies a commanding position in his bedroom. "Friends found it for me and I love it. But I often wonder which is worth more, the mirror or the Andy Warhol auction stickers on the back of it."

Axelrod has amassed his treasury of art in a relatively short time by tapping many sources and taking many routes to acquire the art he wants. When he began to acquire the California ceramics that enliven his starkly dramatic living room, he went directly to the artists and was offered his choice of works from the studios of ceramicists like Peter Voulkos and Viola Fry. However, he also buys at auction houses and from dealers, "some of whom I trust completely and others whom I deal with just because I want what they're selling," he says. "In those situations, I do a lot more research. I work with dealers in Buenos Aires when I'm looking for Latin

In Axelrod's study, a Wells Fargo desk and William Morris wallpaper create a romantic setting for the Uruguayan and Argentinian paintings hung from eye level to ceiling. On the mantel is an idiosyncratic display of art objects—Augusta Savage's bust of John Henry, ten centuries of Thai buddhas, and "grotesque" vases made by slaves.

23

One wall in Axelrod's entrance hall is devoted to Brazilian, Uruguayan, and African-American paintings, as well as a grouping (right) of five social realist works. A Peter Voulkos ceramic urn sits next to an Eli Jacques Kahn Art Deco cabinet serving as a pedestal for various sculptures.

American art. In New York, I discovered the Michael Rosenfeld Gallery because it has become a new force in African-American art. I brought home nine paintings from their first show of twentieth-century African-American masterworks in 1993 and several since then, including my most recent prize by Hale Woodruff. It's the painting I mention a lot these days because when I'm asked, as happens frequently, what's my favorite piece, I always answer, the last thing I bought."

Axelrod has spent the last quarter of a century building diverse collections, several of which he has given or loaned to the Boston Museum of Fine Arts and Yale University. "My home has a finite capacity, and I decided I can't add without subtracting. For the most part, I won't buy something new without making room for it."

IAN & MARY DUNLOP

I SOMETIMES LONG FOR A MONASTIC SPACE
BUT CAN NEVER ACHIEVE IT.

This place is a reflection of the history of my life with art, which goes back thirty years," says Ian Dunlop, looking around the small London apartment he shares with his wife, Mary, and their son, Rory. Ian's art life began in the late 1950s at Trinity College, Dublin, where he wrote a piece about the Irish artist Jack Yeats, brother of the poet William B. Yeats, for a local magazine. His first purchase was a Yeats drawing which cost 50 pounds—"quite a lot for me, at least two months' allowance." Despite a continuing lack of cash, this was the beginning of a life unequivocally committed to art. "In those years I would say it was more important to have paintings than comfort. Now I'm not so sure!" he says.

Ian Dunlop moved to London in the early 1960s and, after a stint at the London *Times*, became art critic for the *Evening Standard*, the city's major evening paper. "It was a golden period for contemporary art," he recalls. "Hockney, Kitaj, Bridget Riley—I immmediately responded to this art, and bought Hockney and Kenneth Noland works

that were then still affordable. My parents were shocked by my early collecting and used to tease me about my strange taste." Ian found himself in the center of the explosive art world of the sixties in London, centered around the Kasmin Gallery, where new artists were often given their first shows. "I knew artists and what was going on," Ian says. "It was a marvelous time." During that period, he also bought Indian miniatures on the advice of artist Howard Hodgkin, a longtime collector.

But the good times did not last. Money was in short supply, and to his everlasting regret, Ian later had to sell the Hockney drawings and the Noland. (He still has photographs of them.) In 1973 he joined Sotheby's and moved to the United States. Plunging into the American contemporary art world, he fell in love with the work of Ed Ruscha and Richard Diebenkorn, among others. He also became enthusiastic about Egyptian sculpture and nineteenth-century bronzes. In New York he worked briefly as a private art dealer, specializing in architectural and natural history drawings, including the work of

OPPOSITE

The comfortable and relaxed air of the Dunlops' London living room is derived from what Ian calls an "eclectic mishmash" of nineteenth- and twentieth-century European artists, along with natural history drawings and Indian miniatures.

Elizabeth Butterworth ("the best living painter of parrots and birds,"), Donald Sultan, and Avigdor Arikha. "All these are my friends," he says.

After his marriage to Mary MacDougal, her possessions were added to the mix, both furniture and pictures, mostly inherited from her family, such as a portrait by Cecil Beaton of her grandmother with her three daughters. In 1987 the Dunlops finally moved back to England. "It's an eclectic mishmash," Ian concedes, looking round the drawing room of their crowded London flat, where the Indian miniatures he managed not to sell ("I have an abiding interest in Indian art") hang beside Edwardian paintings, English and Scottish watercolors, modern art, and contemporary photographs. "The eye tends to roam around the room. We let people choose what they want to look at," he says.

Ian dreams of a different kind of space, though. "There is so much English clutter here. I sometimes long for a monastic space but can never achieve it. For instance, if I had all the money in the world, I would love to have a very contemporary belvedere or flat devoted to contemporary art on a large scale, such as the work of Damien Hirst or Hiroshi Sugimoto. It's easy to fall in love instantaneously with an artist like Hockney. These days I am more interested in art that initially puts me off and then gradually I see the logic of it."

He is now concentrating on contemporary photography, which is on a smaller scale than, say, Hirst, but still gives him the visual challenge he demands from a work of art. "I can't stop buying," he admits, "although it's always on a budget. The great thing about photography is that it is still affordable and it does not require so much wall space." Then he adds, sighing, "Collecting is an obsessive instinct. I suppose I am always looking for that buzz."

Early nineteenth-century French portraits and a set of English Views near Smyrna add atmosphere to the dining room, which demonstrates that a richly colored wallcovering can enhance the art.

RALPH ESMERIAN

FOLK ART REPRESENTED TO ME . . . ART THAT WAS CLOSE TO THE EARTH.

This is the story of one man's cultural journey from the jeweled walls of his ancient country to the austerity of the New World, from the glittering sophistication of Byzantium to the naive enthusiasm of early America. It's a long journey, but Ralph Esmerian's artistic sense, nurtured by a demanding father and long study, has led him to the place in art, and in the world, where he wishes to dwell.

The Esmerian family emigrated from Constantinople to Paris in the late nineteenth century. Ralph was born in Paris, but his mother was American, and in 1940 the family made their way to New York City. Ralph's father, Raphael, like his father before him, was a dealer in precious stones as well as a lapidary—a cutter specializing in colored stones—and a designer of fine jewelry.

"It didn't mean much to us," Ralph remembers. "My father didn't encourage us to take an interest in his work. This was unusual, perhaps, but I think he felt that his was a medieval trade, and he wanted us to have a modern education in the New World.

Unsure of what he wanted to do after college, Ralph began teaching at Athens College in Greece. After a foray

into urban planning in New York, he finally went to work for his father, who was thinking of retiring. "Suddenly I saw my father in a completely different light," Ralph recalls. "It was a revelation." Instead of a distant parent, his father became an inspired teacher and mentor who introduced his son to the world of rubies, sapphires, emeralds, and diamonds, the precious stones that had been part of the family culture for generations. "For fourteen years I watched and worked with him and then I was hooked. No more illusions about urban planning. I suppose it was in my Byzantine blood that I should ultimately respond so powerfully to the colors and shapes of brilliant gems."

But while returning to the fold, Ralph also began to strike out on his own. For while daily handling the most luxurious, refined, and desirable objects of human decoration, he chose not to surround himself with the Eastern or European paintings and sculptures that corresponded to this opulent universe, but instead became drawn to the naive, simple pictures, furniture, and utensils of nineteenth-century America.

"I started because of a friend who loved early American things. I wanted to get her a present and went to a folk art dealer to buy something for her. He had a piece of nineteenth-century pottery like the Greek pottery I had collected in Athens. I bought it at once."

From then on, Ralph studied every aspect of American folk art. He looked at it in museums. He visited shops and dealers in New England and Pennsylvania. He endured the disapproval of his father, who heaped scorn on his son's new passion. But Ralph persevered. "I was working in this ultrasophisticated business of rare gemstones," he explains, "and folk art represented to me the opposite, art that was close to the earth, springing from the souls of people trying to earn a living and bringing practical beauty into their dreary daily lives."

Another impulse that inspired Esmerian stemmed from the immigrant experience. "As I traveled around, I learned that for many immigrants the United States

is paradise. It is where people want to come. That made me want to celebrate this country's early art, almost as an expression of gratitude."

Esmerian's New York apartment reflects that American bias. Its several small rooms are furnished almost entirely in nineteenth-century American arts and crafts—primitive paintings, painted furniture, quilts, and pottery. Only in the heavy damask curtains and upholstery and in the jewel-like

RIGHT

The walls of the bedroom are covered with early American portraits and landscapes. The portrait on the right is of the Farwell children of Pittsburgh, Massachusetts, painted in 1841.

BELOW

In the hall is a charming portrait of Jonathan Knight, founder of Yale Medical School, painted by an unknown artist in 1797.

30

density of the multifaceted patterns and objects is there perhaps some reminder of Esmerian's history. Indeed, there seems not an inch of room to spare. Would he consider moving to a larger space? Absolutely not. This is the perfect expression of his adopted country. However, in the near future, the collection will go to the new Museum of American Folk Art being built in New York City.

In 1978, Ralph Esmerian became president of the Museum of American Folk Art. He is also the owner of one of the most famous paintings ever to come out of that tradition: *Peaceable Kingdom* by Edward Hicks. Ralph first saw the painting in the Kennedy Galleries and longed for it, but could not afford it. He instead persuaded his father, who was beginning to collect American impressionists, to buy it. In 1976, a week before Raphael Esmerian died, he told his son the painting was his.

CLARE & EUGENE THAW

ART GIVES A FOCUS
TO EVERYTHING YOU DO.

To enter the Thaws' two-story maisonette, disguised within a New York City highrise, is to be reminded of the private art collections that were destined to become museums. The visitor is transported to another time and place. The effect is startling, since many of the rooms appear to reflect the art-filled European interiors depicted in the nineteenth-century watercolors that welcome visitors in the entry hall of the Thaw home.

Period furniture is arranged to encourage contemplation of art in every room. Tables are covered with small oil sketches and finely wrought objects from the late Middle Ages to the twentieth century, and eyes are drawn to cabinets and walls of books and catalogs. The lighting is deliberately dimmed for the preservation of the drawings. "I keep everything in the gloom here," Gene explains. "There is enough illumination for me to see the drawings. I'm not showing them off. I just want to know that they are here."

Gene's arrangements of wall art and objects become still life vignettes. He is intensely involved in the mounting, framing, and hanging of each piece of art, rearranging rooms as his collections grow and travel to museums. "I change the art around whenever I feel like it," he says. "Sometimes I stay up late when I sense that things should have a different juxtaposition."

Gene explains, "One of the joys of life is to assemble and order something that ends up having true meaning and to share it and show it to others who have some glimmering of what you are doing. The end should be more than a good auction catalog." Thaw recalls that when he was a young art dealer in the 1950s, his wife, Clare, encouraged him to give what they were doing some deeper meaning by collecting only art that would qualify for museum exhibition and acquisition. They succeeded. In just forty years, Eugene and Clare have filled their New York and New Mexico homes with not one but three diverse collections of historical importance.

In 1995 Clare and Gene Thaw donated 250 coveted old master drawings to the Pierpont Morgan Library. Three exhibitions followed in New York with a fourth in London when the Royal Academy of Arts selected one

OPPOSITE

The Thaws enlisted the late Mark Hampton to create a dining room with a Victorian atmosphere. With a bow to Henry McIlhenny, he lined the walls with plaid fabric, an unusual backdrop for the Thaws' watercolor interiors and the eighteenth-century G. B. Tiepolo sketch for a ceiling mural centered on the far wall.

Eugene Thaw rests in the corner of his living room where he has arranged a much-prized group of late eighteenth- and early nineteenth-century en-plein-air landscapes by Corot, Michallon, and three of the nine lost Valenciennes he recently acquired.

hundred Thaw drawings from Mantegna to Picasso for their tremendous presence and wall-power.

34

After buying a house in Santa Fe in the late 1980s, Clare discovered a beadwork American flag, which inspired their second collection—American Indian art. Four years later, when the walls, tables, and shelves in their New Mexico home could no longer contain it all, the Thaws donated 700 pieces, dating from prehistoric times to the present, to the New York State Historical Association's Fenimore House Museum in Cooperstown.

For more than three decades the Thaws also collected watercolors of nineteenth-century interiors. These images of a vanished way of life are especially cherished by Clare, whose aesthetic sensibility is evident in the decor of their New York and Santa Fe homes. Charles Ryskamp, director of the Frick Museum, exhibited this

Thaw's study preserves the memory of the master drawings he gave to the Morgan Library. Works by Delacroix, Géricault, Corot, Ingres, and Degas mounted in French-lined mattes are arranged on a brown-beige cloth wall. On the desk, an eighteenth-century oil sketch by Guardi.

The Thaws' inviting entryhall is richly hung with watercolors from their collection of nineteenth-century interiors. Arranged on an eighteenth-century table are Chinese porcelain vases and an architectural model made for them by Viscount David Linley.

36

charming collection in 1992. Several of these watercolors appear on pages 42–45.

Although the Thaws have given away much of their art, their home remains a rich testament to their passion for drawings—and represents a role call of celebrated draftsmen over the last three hundred years. Seated at a desk in his study, Gene faces the works of twentieth-century masters: Picasso, Cézanne, Léger, Matisse, Klee, and Ernst. Across the hall is a sitting room that contains Thaw's latest acquisition, the nine lost works of Valenciennes, an eighteenth-century artist whose other plein air drawings can be seen only in the Louvre. Gene points out two Corots positioned on easels facing the Valenciennes explaining with great excitement that Valenciennes is considered "the grandfather of Corot's style. . . .

"It is the aesthetic impact of the drawings themselves and not the discovery that turns me on," Thaw says. "It is their particular quality and kinship to handwriting which most attracts me to them. In this age of computers, mul-tiples, and duplication, the artist's hand seems to be getting less important. All the more reason to cherish such survivals from other times when the hand of genius was a sign of civilization."

Gene credits Clare with igniting his passion for collecting master drawings. Their first major purchase, an 1890 Gauguin monotype, is now the centerpiece of the upstairs viewing room. "We bought it with a borrowed $5,000 in 1955. Though the pride of my collection is now at the Morgan, this is still a good room," Gene says.

"Art gives a focus to everything you do," Thaw says. "In collecting, the trial-and-error approach is best. It's an intellectual activity in which one makes deliberate choices and takes some risks. European paintings and drawings are not the only things in the world today. There are hundreds of other things—ceramics, for example. It is important to have a good eye as well as an adviser or guru. It certainly helps to listen to dealers, read books, travel, visit galleries and museums." Thaw relates the story of an American "lost soul" he met in Florence who asked him, "What is there to do in this town?" Gene says, "I simply pointed the man in the direction of the Uffizi."

Gene Thaw collects multiple examples by artists who illuminate his understanding of draftsmanship in western art. In his viewing room he grouped a painting of a woman and two self-portraits by Degas. Seventeenth-century Italian and Flemish bronzes grace the mantel.

Eugene Thaw describes his living room, filled with eighteenth- and nineteenth-century antique furniture, as an American translation of English country style. The walls were painted gray-blue, a palette that works well with the landscape oil sketches hanging there.

MARY JANE HARRIS

I HAD NEVER BEEN IN THE PRESENCE OF AN OLD MASTER PAINTING.

How violent!" "How strange!" Mary Jane Harris is amused by such responses to her art. For her, these seventeenth- and eighteenth-century Italian baroque paintings are her life, "my raison d'être."

How she began is as baroque a story as the art. In 1963, on vacation in Sarasota, Florida, with her late husband, Morton, they took refuge during a rainstorm in the Ringling Museum of Art, where there was an exhibition of Genoese baroque paintings in progress. For Mary Jane, it was a revelation. "I had never been in the presence of an old master painting," she said. "It was second love at first sight." (The first was Morton.)

This confrontation in Sarasota was as dramatic for her as Saul's on the road to Damascus. Not that she rushed out to the nearest dealer and started making purchases. Mrs. Harris was a lingerie buyer in New York. She wanted to learn more about her new discovery, but she was also on a very limited budget. Three years later, after auditing art history courses after work and studying with experts, she bought her first old master drawing, a Simone Pignoni (circa 1670).

By 1967, she was completely focused. She became a friend of collector Paul Ganz, and the Harrises' first important picture, Guercino's *St. Jerome,* came from him. The other big acquisition at that time was *David with the Head of Goliath* by Gerolamo Forabosco, which the Harrises had seen in Venice. When it arrived in New York and was uncrated in their living room, Mary Jane was so moved that she wept.

In these years, the Harrises were living in a small apartment in Stuyvesant Town, not exactly ideal for these huge canvases. They moved to a large apartment on New York's Upper West Side, where furnishings took a modest second place to the art. The pictures have been—and still are—the dominant visual feature of the decor. And what did Morton think of all this? "He was long-suffering, but he never stood in my way. He gave me an art allowance each year to supplement my salary. The deal was that I could have the art—but no family!"

Mary Jane Harris bought steadily for about a decade. Because the subjects of Italian baroque painting—severed heads, fainting Madonnas, blood-soaked saints—are not particularly appealing to the taste of many Americans,

OPPOSITE

Glorious seventeenth-century Italian works grace the hall: On the left,
Santa Reperata *by Simone Pignoni; center,* Sacra Conversazione *by*
Cecco Bravo; *right,* Penitent Magdalene *by Giovanni Battista*
Lupicini; *over the fireplace, a* Bacchanale *by Livio Mehus.*

the Harrises in the sixties and early seventies could buy great works for several thousand dollars. "Not that I was motivated by commercial considerations," she says. "It never occurred to me that some people might object to martyrdoms in the dining room." For her, the collection is about light, sensuality, and spirituality.

Mary Jane is now well respected in the field. Curators and collectors consult her for her opinions and attributions. Today, baroque paintings of high quality are becoming increasingly expensive. "I can't afford to buy much anymore," she says. "But now I am not thinking about accumulation. I am thinking instead about

where the collection will eventually be placed." (Her alma mater, Penn State University, will be one of the lucky recipients.)

While a connoisseur of the baroque, Mary Jane has expanded her taste to include the High Renaissance and Mannerism, and nineteenth- and twentieth-century drawings. But her deepest commitment remains to the glorious art that exploded on her consciousness all those years ago in Sarasota. Looking back, she makes this observation for the young collector: "Buy against taste. Have conviction—and a companion who loves you."

LEFT

Of Judith with Holofernes *by Gregorio Lozzarini (Venice, 1655–1730) hanging in the dining room, Mary Jane Harris says, "I find it thrilling."*

ABOVE

In the simply furnished living room, Mary Jane Harris's most prized painting, a portrait of Saint Jerome by Guercino dated 1637, glows as though lit from within. On the right, a work by Charles Antoine Coypel, dated 1740.

BEFORE OUR TIME

NINETEENTH-CENTURY ART-FILLED ROOMS

In the early nineteenth century, proud European home-owners revived the tradition of interior portraiture and immortalized their homes by commissioning paintings of entrance halls, salons, libraries, studies, drawing rooms, and bedrooms. Originally gathered in elaborately bound portfolios, these watercolors provide charming, vivid views of formal arrangements of furniture, profusely

patterned floor and wall coverings, and an idiosyncratic mix of objects and art—historical masterpieces, classical sculpture, and family miniatures and memorabilia.

These watercolors from Eugene Thaw's collection, which illuminate the history of taste in nineteenth-century interior design, were borrowed from his home for a 1992 exhibition at the Frick Collection. Charlotte Gere, author of the museum catalog, wrote, "The idea that the contents of a room and their arrangement might be the expression of an individual personality and thus artistically interesting must have been behind the impulse that produced these paintings."

In contrasting these nineteenth-century watercolor interiors with photographs of the twentieth-century

ABOVE

An Interior with a Curtained Bed Alcove (1850s)

The elegant decoration and curtained sleeping alcove in this bedroom-boudoir suggest that it was used to receive guests. The walls are densely hung with pictures. Other works are displayed on the writing table and on a two-tiered easel that faces the light. This painting is presumed to be the work of an anonymous Austrian painter.

LEFT

A Salon in the Empire Taste (fl. 1820s)

French and Dutch seventeenth- and eighteenth-century romantic land-scapes and interior scenes dominate this salon thought to be painted by H. Thierry. The arrangement of these closely hung paintings in two rows barely above eye level was called a "Dutch cabinet hang." Conspicuous among them is a moonlit seascape by Claude-Joseph Vernet (or imitator).

art-filled rooms in this book, a question arises: how will the next wave of plugged-in, technology-driven art challenge and reshape our concepts of aesthetics and interior design? Just as the canvases and sculpture of the modern era inspired and required many art lovers to maximize wall space, minimize furniture, and paint their walls gallery white, so will the art of the new millennium, whatever it may be, have a profound impact on where and how we live with art.

44

ABOVE

A Salon in a Residence of the Duke of Leuchtenberg (1850)
Close-hung portraits were common in the private rooms of palaces, whereas public rooms were often hung with old masters. Landscapist Otto Wagner's painting of this salon reveals portraits with different frame styles, suggesting they came from the German, Russian, and French family collections of the Duke and Duchess of Leuchtenberg.

OPPOSITE

Room in the Reuss Palace, Dresden (1835/37)
Like many exiled families in nineteenth-century Poland, C. M. Fredro (thought to be the artist of this picture) and his mother may have rented this modest room in one of the princely palaces. The small unframed drawings were mounted on a screen and in the window embrasure so as not to damage the costly decorative wall covering.

Research for captions was generously provided by Charlotte Gere, author of 19th Century Interiors: An Album of Watercolors (Thames & Hudson, 1992), an authority on decoration of this period.

DIGRESSION ON *NUMBER 1, 1948*

FRANK O'HARA

I am ill today but I am not

too ill. I am not ill at all.

It is a perfect day, warm

for winter, cold for fall.

A fine day for seeing. I see

ceramics, during lunch hour by

Miró and I see the sea by Léger;

Light, complicated Metzingers

and a rude awakening by Brauner,

a little table by Picasso, pink.

I am tired today but I am not

too tired. I am not tired at all.

There is the Pollock, white, harm

will not fall, his perfect hand

and the many short voyages. They'll

never fence the silver range.

Stars are out and there is sea

enough beneath the glistening earth

to bear me toward the future

which is not so dark. I see.

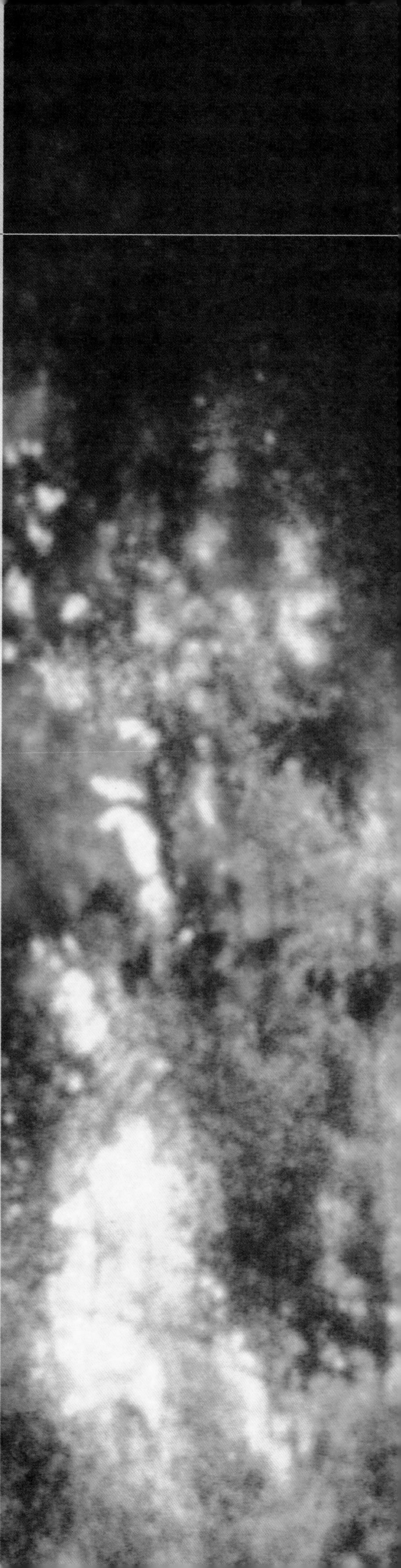

THE FOCUSED EYE

ROZ & MEL JACOBS

I FELL IN LOVE WITH THE PEOPLE

AND THEN THE ART.

Like the art of Man Ray, the surrealist Roz Jacobs most admires, her duplex apartment amuses, bewilders, provokes, and inspires reflection. "When people come into my home, they are taken by surprise," she says. "Nobody seems to think it's strange, but I have a lot of explaining to do. They enjoy discovering the art, even as I did. Best of all, they like knowing this art was done with a sense of humor."

The surrealist art environment that she and her late husband, Mel Jacobs, created reflects careers that were dependent on "discovery of the new." Visionary merchants, Roz and Mel worked independently but saw eye to eye on the art they wanted to live with. "We moved in a visually exciting world of fashion and design and developed an affinity for art that challenged the boundaries of reality. Surrealism was not new when we discovered it in the fifties, but it was new to us," Roz explains. "My attraction to it was immediate; it stretched my imagination."

The element of chance inherent in surrealist art was present when Roz Jacobs, a young fashion director for R. H. Macy, went off to view the Paris collections in

1955. A fortuitous meeting with gallery owner Sidney Janis led her to the home of American expatriate artist William Copley. He and his wife Noma introduced her to many of the "upstarts in the artistic community at the time—the surrealists," among them Man Ray and his wife, Julie, who became lifelong friends. "I fell in love with

ABOVE

Roz Jacobs stands mirrored in her entryway next to her favorite Man Ray photograph, the original Violon d'Ingres *(1924). A devotee of surrealist jewelry, she wears a silver necktie by Noma Copley.*

OPPOSITE

An outsized Fornasetti platter casts watchful eyes over a kitchen door leading to an entry hall with quixotic art and furniture. Arman's light bulb chandelier illuminates a curiously Byzantine Martial Raysee portrait, a Victorian hall porter's chair, a faux parcel post ceramic box, and walls of Man Ray art.

OVERLEAF

The Jacobses closed off a wall in their dining room to make space for a 1983 Gilbert & George photo piece, View. *Table settings and decor continue the surrealist theme: a William Copley screen, Man Ray's centerpiece,* Blue Bread, *and Fornasetti serving plates, which are also used as displays.*

A sinister 1952 Matta oil, Being Beauteous, *is underlined by an arrangement of whimsical surrealist sculptures on the fireplace mantel.*

the people and then the art," Roz says. "The surrealists were fun people to be with. Life was the butt of the joke.

"Most of the artists we acquired we discovered through the Copleys," she explains. "They were extremely influential in helping us understand and appreciate surrealist art. The first piece of art I ever acquired was a gift from them, a Magritte gouache *[L'Éloge de la Dialectique]* that I had admired in their home. It was just so beautiful, I longed for it. It became the adventure of my life when it slipped out of its envelope at Orly airport, turning up in the lost-and-found two weeks later." The gouache is now one of two Magrittes that bracket the fireplace in Roz Jacobs's living room. "It influenced everything we collected from then on. We only bought things that spoke to us, never thinking of their future value.

"We deliberately chose comfortable, unobtrusive couches and chairs, wanting to create a relaxed atmosphere without upstaging the art. Mel arranged most of the art himself. He decided we had to close up the kitchen to

create a wall large enough for one of our more recent acquisitions, a Gilbert & George photo-realist mural that now dominates our dining room." And Roz remembers with amusement that Mel deliberately positioned a Dorothea Tanning painting over the couch at a right angle to Max Ernst's portrait of Peggy Guggenheim. Ernst had been married to both of them.

Evidence of Man Ray, the painter, the photographer, the object maker, can be found throughout the house. As you enter, your eyes are immediately drawn to Man Ray's *Violon d'Ingres,* the portrait of his muse, Kiki of Montparnasse. "I was very upset with Man Ray when this photograph suddenly appeared everywhere, and people kept telling me that theirs was an original silver print," Roz explains. "I complained to Man Ray, but he assured me I had the original and a scratch mark on the print was proof of it. Then with characteristic mischief, he sent me a poster promoting a Man Ray show featuring this image and wrote across it, 'To create is divine, to reproduce is human.'"

At the top of the staircase is a framed series of Man Ray silkscreens from his *Revolving Doors* portfolio. A collection of nineteenth-century flatirons, inspired by the artist's notorious flatiron studded with nails, marches up the staircase. "Soon after we met," Roz remembers, "Man took me through the catacombs and later I watched him buy ten flatirons from an antique shop that he painted red and called *Le Fer Rouge*—the red-hot iron. I bought one, and ever since, whenever I'm traveling, I try to bring one home to add to the collection."

The fireplace mantel has become an altar celebrating surrealist art. An arrangement of miniature sculptures includes pieces by Martinazzi and Niki de Saint Phalle,

The Jacobses' living room has wit and warmth. Magritte paintings frame the fireplace. Arman created the amusing base for their coffee table. The piano becomes a pedestal for Duchamp's unfolding valise and an ostrich egg Man Ray called "the most perfect of human shapes."

Duchamp's famed *Feuille de Vigne,* as well as Man Ray's smoking device and metronome, an improvised collaboration with William Copley, constructed at a dinner party. Centered on the wall above the mantel and serving as counterpoint to these whimsical artworks is a Matta oil, *Being Beauteous,* which Roz interprets as "the man who wants to devour everything." Roz and Mel bought this painting in the 1960s from New York art dealer Alexandre Iolas. "We didn't see it as a political statement when we bought it," Roz says. "It just appealed to us. We trusted Iolas's extraordinary eye and thought of him as an art mentor and a good friend. Knowing I was headed for Brussels and passionate to meet Magritte, he gave me a check to deliver to the artist."

Roz points to the unicorn gouache she bought from Magritte during that first meeting. "Touring his Victorian house I braved the question, 'Why do you paint so many things over and over again?' His answer changed the way I thought about painting: 'Some ideas are just so important, they have to be repeated.'"

53

The portrait over the sofa in the Duncans' glowing living room, painted
by an unknown Italian artist in 1832, was bought by Mimi's grandfather in Europe, "because it looked like a friend of hers."

MIMI & RUSSELL DUNCAN

I COULDN'T HAVE A THREE-NOSED PICASSO IN MY LIVING ROOM.

Mimi and Russell Duncan live in a delightful six-story tower just off Worth Avenue in Palm Beach, Florida. The building was built in 1919 by the architect Addison Mizner for the American sewing-machine millionaire Paris Singer. Mizner, who created the Spanish-style architecture and ambience of Palm Beach, lived nearby in a twin tower. The surrounding area resembles a Mediterranean village, with meandering alleyways running into pretty courtyards enclosed in white stucco walls topped by red tile roofs. Fountains and outdoor restaurants add to the charm, along with shops and apartments designed like miniature medieval castles, with balconies and wrought-iron grillwork.

The interior of the Duncans' tower has a southern flavor, since many of the artworks and antique furnishings were inherited by Mimi, who comes from Memphis, Tennessee. "I grew up in Memphis," Mimi says. "And when we moved to Palm Beach, I brought my family treasures with me. My father was on the board of the Brooks Museum, and my mother was one of the founders of the Memphis Academy of Art, so the interest comes naturally. Russell and I both appreciate art and have added to the collection over the years."

Mimi met her future husband in Rome soon after the war, where he was working with the Marshall Plan. They became engaged in Trieste a few months later.

"There we had the opportunity to pick up some really good pictures at reasonable prices," Mimi recalls. Russell Duncan comes from Arizona, and in addition to painting quite skillfully himself, he reveals his roots in one of the guest sitting rooms, which has a fine

On a marble-topped table are a group of personal favorites, including an interior of Dunrobin Castle by Lord Berners, a domestic scene by Pedro Figari, a sketch by Edwina Sandys, and a portrait of Mimi by Elizabeth Martin.

collection of western art. One might say there is a dual theme running through the Duncan household— Memphis meets Tucson, to everyone's satisfaction.

Looking round these cozy rooms, one sees evidence everywhere of Mimi's sense of home. The colors on the walls, for instance, are bright and confident, well able to handle the strong Florida sunlight and at the same time a good background for the pictures. The warmth of the furniture and furnishings, and the wide range of paintings on each of the six floors of the tower, make this a very personal place to visit.

In the Duncans' house the saying "Every picture tells a story" is true. "I bought my first painting in Oak Street on Chicago," Mimi remembers, "and we still have it hanging over our living room mantel. We raised our children in New York City, and I acquired pictures there too, as I went along." A sketch in a guest room, done by Russell Duncan at a dinner party, won him a bottle of champagne. Some years ago, while visiting in Tucson, Mimi and Russell discovered a very talented Mexican artist called Romo working in poverty. They bought a painting and went back to buy others, but the artist had mysteriously disappeared. "It was very sad for us. When we buy something, we want to follow up." Mimi is currently very enthusiastic about Edith Caywood, a young Memphis painter, who does interiors that remind Mimi of her childhood.

Mimi cheerfully admits that her art collecting is "highly decorative. I couldn't have a three-nosed Picasso in my living room." For example, she fell in love with a large Léon Bakst painting she saw twenty years ago in London and bought it, guessing the colors would be perfect in her dining room back home. She was right.

56

In the brilliantly colored dining room, the large painting by Léon Bakst, better known for his costume designs for the Ballets Russes, is a striking presence above Mimi's silver collection. The painting on the far wall is by Serge Hollerbach.

JOHN & JUNE HECHINGER

HAMMERS, WRENCHES, SCREWS, SCREWDRIVERS, ARE BEAUTIFUL IN THEMSELVES. THROUGH AN ARTIST'S VISION THEY BECOME AESTHETIC OBJECTS.

If I had been on the jury that rejected Marcel Duchamp's scandalous *Fountain,* a signed porcelain urinal exhibited in 1917, I would have voted to accept it," John Hechinger explains. "In the hands of an artist, the ordinary can become extraordinary."

John and June Hechinger's Washington, D.C., home exalts the tools and materials used to make a house. "Hammers, wrenches, ladders, screws, screwdrivers, and lawn mowers are beautiful in themselves," John says, "and through an artist's vision they become aesthetic objects that make a house even more beautiful." So saying, he leads visitors to paintings, prints, photographs, and sculptures by Claes Oldenburg, Fernand Léger, Jim Dine, Arman, Berenice Abbott, and others that illustrate this, as does the house itself. Walter Gropius didn't know when he designed a classically modern home for John and June in 1950 that he was creating an appropriate environment for their amusing collection of "utilitarian art."

It all began in 1978, when John Hechinger conceived the idea that art devoted to tools could give the employees of his company, a chain of Home Center stores, pride in their work and "the pedestrian products they handled every day. I started looking for this art with a single-minded, laserlike focus." He hung Jim Dine's *Tool Box* in his corporate headquarters, and the response it stirred up encouraged him to build a collection of more than 350 works of art celebrating the "dignity and beauty of hardware." The works proved enormously popular when they were shown in 1995 at the National Building Museum in Washington, D.C. Curator Caroline Laray wrote in the book that commemorates the event, "What at first appears to be a theme of narrow focus, is, to the contrary, one that provides a vibrant and rich path for artistic exploration by an extraordinary range of artists.

While Hechinger concentrated at first on renowned postwar artists, he also discovered many works by emerging artists of the last quarter of the twentieth century. Several of them challenge the viewer's perception of reality and demonstrate the pleasure John derives from discovering an artist who sees a conventional product in unconventional proportions and materials. There is Hans Godo Frabel's startling sculpture of a hammer and nails

OPPOSITE

The Hechingers planned defined areas for a surprising juxtaposition of tool and folk art. Granny, a figure from a candy store window, sits in front of a glass table displaying Still Hungry, a cluster of wrenches by Arman. A sculpture made by a Tennessee woodsman guards a glass wall protecting biscuit and tobacco tins.

made of glass and a towering drill bit made of wood.

As he gathered artworks to enhance the identity of his company, John was signaling his own identity with what he calls "the tools of the trade" by sending some of his favorite artworks home. Several paintings and prints by Jim Dine, the first artist whose work John bought, are prominently displayed in the Hechinger home. A suite of ten colored lithographs, each a portrait of a different tool, is arranged so they can be admired in the living room and seen close up on the way to the bedroom. The door to John and June's bedroom is ornamented by a one-of-a-kind Fernand Léger doorknob.

Many works by Arman, a sculptor Hechinger describes as "an accumulator," fill the house, starting at the front door where his *Avalanche,* a group of axes, sets the stage for what's inside. Arman's bouquet of wrenches

A Michael Malpass globe made out of salvaged parts and construction materials is the focal point of the living room. It anchors a table arranged with Chris Collicott's steel Wrench Bowl, *an oversized screw by Mineo Mizuno, and Hans Godo Frabel's glass hammer and nails.*

Debra Chase's wire-mesh jacket brings startling beauty into the Hechinger bathroom. It reveals a ghostly pattern of hand tools.

is positioned perilously on a glass-top coffee table, in jarring contrast with a folk sculpture Hechinger calls "Granny, the candy store lady. Like the barbershop pole," he explains, "she was a sign to customers of what's in store for them. Every once in a while you find something you can't resist. Even though it doesn't connect with the rest of your collection, it does with you, and you must go for it."

Simultaneously, as John sought art that romanticized everyday tools, June was assembling a collection of antique American tobacco and English biscuit tins. "Although I wanted a very contemporary house," June explains, "I found it cold and colorless. The gift of a large orange tobacco tin changed all this and got me started. A few years ago, when I had tins all over the house, we built a wall in the living room for them because John said he was beginning to feel 'boxed in.'" By arranging the tins behind glass and lighting them from within, John and June created the illusion of a collage mural, unifying June's early-twentieth-century folk art collection with John's modern works.

Although they were unaware of it at the time, John and June were taking complementary journeys that would glorify the ordinary objects of their individual worlds. Their art evokes a nostalgic view of a time when men went to work with their toolboxes and women were at home making the cookies and confections they would store in decorative tin boxes. Twenty years ago

Tools of the trade were carved and painted by Ed McGowin to frame his Workers Waving Goodbye. *On the right is a 5½ foot tall wood screwdriver sculpted by F. L. Wall. "It's like an icon in a church," John says.*

John discovered the first of several Michael Malpass globes he would acquire. Salvaged bronze, brass, copper, and steel parts and pieces were interlocked to create a glistening sphere. One of them stands as a centerpiece in the Hechingers' living room, a metaphor for the seamless marriage of John and June's passion for art and craft.

HARRY VAN DYKE

WE WANTED THINGS THAT WERE APPROPRIATE FOR A NINETEENTH-CENTURY HUDSON VALLEY HOME.

Harry van Dyke remembers shopping with his grandmother in Albany, New York, when he was six years old and falling in love with a picture in an antique store window. His grandmother said to the owner, "My grandson would like that picture. How much does it cost?" "The woman turned to me," van Dyke says, "and asked, 'How much do you have?' I reached into my pocket and took out a nickel. 'That's exactly the price,' she said." Van Dyke still has that painting, and it's prominently displayed on the staircase landing of his home in the Hudson Valley. It is a portrait of a man painted by a local Albany artist, Thurston W. Black, in 1862.

His precocious appreciation for regional historical art signaled the course his life would take. Van Dyke, who became an architect dedicated to the restoration of historic homes, talks of the influence of ancestral roots that link him to the cultural legacy of early New York State and his commitment to preserve the richness of its architecture, art, artifacts, and furniture. His ancestors were among the first settlers of Manhattan in 1640, later following other Dutch colonists to Albany. The van Dykes

remained there for four generations until Harry moved downriver in 1960 with his brother, Frank, and their mother. They bought the 1832 Livingston family residence, Forth House, one of the great Greek Revival brick houses in America.

Harry and Frank, a horticulturist who created the gardens and conservatory on the grounds, bought much of the art they lived with together. "When we started out, we were not looking for pictures of cowboys and Indians. We were not looking for French impressionists.

Lithographs of the first ten presidents, Washington to John Tyler, line the staircase wall. On the landing is a bust of George Washington below the 1862 portrait by Albany painter Thurston W. Black that van Dyke bought as a boy.

ABOVE

Van Dyke and his dogs, Emily and Tilly, on the porch of his 1832 Greek Revival house.

We wanted art, furniture, and decorative objects that were handsome, available, and appropriate for a nineteenth-century Hudson Valley home."

The van Dykes looked for and chose art and furniture that fit into the historical context of their landmark house. "You have to have something to sit on and something on the walls and on the floor," Harry explains. "My architectural experience enabled me to coordinate all elements harmoniously." As he says this, Harry leads you outside to view the unique collection of nineteenth-century American black cast-iron decorative pieces he and his brother collected for the lawn and entrance of Forth House. (Frank died in 1997, but Harry talks about him as if he were still alive.)

Harry often describes the artist's connection to the Hudson Valley as a reason for choosing an artwork. "We favored primarily local things," he says, leading you to a painting by Thomas Cole who lived right across the river. "We bought it from his grand-niece. It's a view of Round Top. You get exactly the same view from our upstairs window, so that's the reason we felt it belonged in this house."

The twin parlors in the house are filled with story-telling pictures. There is the 1840 portrait by George Bottume, a Connecticut painter. Harry tells you that it remained unframed for forty years because they couldn't find the right one. "Then we went to an antique sale . . . and found the perfect frame when we weren't even looking for it." Above the Bottume is an 1880 equestrian picture by Harry Sunter that came with the house. "It's a portrait of a woman who would have been the grandmother of the woman we bought this house from," Harry explains. An oil painting by Hudson River artist Arthur Parton remains under its original glass. "When I got the picture I was concerned about protecting it, so I talked to the curators at the Frick. They told me to leave it alone. Since it has never been exposed to air, there is no telling what would happen if we removed the glass." Hanging over the stairs is a collection of rare lithographs

of ten American presidents done by lithographers in the last century: Currier and Ives, Endicott, and H. R. Robinson. "We bought them twenty-five years ago in an art gallery in Maine," he says, "along with a composite picture of the first thirteen presidents that hangs in an upstairs room filled with presidential memorabilia."

Harry emphasizes, "I have always thought that in the right hands, the crafting of furniture can be a true art, so my brother and I looked for authentic period pieces primarily made in New York. We bought an 1825 sofa at a fund-raising auction for the Cooper-Hewitt Museum. I don't think anyone had sat on it in seventy-five years, so when someone did, the silk cracked. We were able to save some of the fabric, and we had it reupholstered." There are other New York pieces—a large table from the 1820s is centered in the sitting room. Its authenticity is validated by "its feet, structure, and surface configuration."

Adding to the diversity of their collection is the eighteenth-century Delftware mounted on the walls of their dining room in homage to their Dutch heritage. Filling a cabinet in the same room is another collection of Staffordshire porcelain plates with views of the Hudson River reproduced from W. H. Bartlett prints of the 1830s. "We stopped looking for more," Harry adds, "when they became so popular we could no longer afford them. . . .

"Finding art that you want to live with has changed

since my brother and I began," Harry laments. "It used to be that you could just buy what you wanted, but now everybody wants art and furniture from this particular period in New York's history. Early on, we would just leave bids at Sotheby's and Christie's, but then there came a time when you had to be there because it had become so competitive. Fortunately, my walls and rooms are pretty much filled now."

OPPOSITE

The double parlor reveals period art and furniture respectful of van Dyke's 1832 house and his ancestral roots. An anonymous eighteenth-century oil is surrounded by a collection of eighteenth-century Delftware recalling his Dutch heritage. Doorways are framed with lead medallions inspired by those in the Erechtheum.

BELOW

Prints of the Albany landscape, an 1850 painting by Bottume, and an equestrian oil that came with the house are hung above an 1825 sofa.

Jason Vass surveys his living room, the floor stacked with posters, most

of which communicate powerful political messages. The boxes on the left

are by artist Adam Rolston.

JASON VASS

I CALL MYSELF A POSTER JUNKIE.

ason Vass lives in a modest ground-floor apartment in Santa Monica, California. He furnished it on a shoestring and painted it white. But the space is alive with interest, for Jason Vass is a poster collector, and he pays his rent—just—by buying and selling these works on paper.

Jason's late father, Gene Vass, was an abstract expressionist painter, and his mother, Joan, is a designer of women's clothes. Jason spent his early childhood in Europe, which gave him his formative visual education.

Jason's adolescence coincided with the political activism of the late 1960s, and he became deeply involved in demonstrations against the Vietnam War. He was an early supporter of underground art, and in the early 1980s became a silent partner in a gallery called 56 Bleecker, where luminaries such as Andy Warhol attended openings. "At that time you could pick up a Robert Mapplethorpe photograph for $500," he recalls, "but nobody bothered. We put Jean-Michel Basquiat in a group show and could hardly give the paintings away."

Disillusioned with the New York art world, Jason finally settled in southern California where he has lived for over seven years now. "I'd been collecting posters off and on ever since 1980," he says. "I had a strong interest in the Spanish Civil War and Art Deco posters—powerful political images." The first poster Jason ever bought indicates his bias. Called *Foire de Paris,* it advertised the 1935

Paris exposition. "It reflected that wonderful spirit prior to the Second World War and the rise of fascism."

He realized that his interest in posters had become a passion. "I call myself a poster junkie. I have had at times over a hundred posters at home and no room to display them." He works mostly with young collectors, who are priced out of other art. "Posters can be acquired from $500 up." And in the ultimate confession of the aficionado, he declares, "I believe posters are really fine art. The line between contemporary art, photography, and posters is almost indefinable. I *love* my posters."

A satin-upholstered Regency chair sounds a different note in Jason's bedroom, with a painting of earth by Alain Jacquet, and a Josephine Baker–inspired poster, Tabarin, *by Paul Colin.*

ERIC ROBERTSON

I SEE CONNECTIONS BETWEEN CULTURES.
THOSE CONNECTIONS INSPIRE ME.

Two themes run through Eric Robertson's life as clearly as the striations on a piece of marble: a social conscience and a love of art. Eric came to the United States from Jamaica in 1949. He became a civil rights organizer in college and, after graduating from law school, worked in Chicago as a Vista Volunteer lawyer. "That gave me my first real taste of big-city politics," he remembers, laughing. But alongside his civil rights activities, he discovered he was constantly being drawn toward the world of art and aesthetics. "Back in Jamaica my cousin was a painter. I remember he painted beautiful potato vines and birds' eggs, images that stayed with me. Also, as a child, I always liked to construct environments. I especially remember a fish tank."

This artistic sensibility lingered. As he became increasingly involved in Chicago's urban affairs, Eric Robertson found himself appreciating the city's buildings more and more. "Chicago has always been a fascinating place architecturally," he says. "During my time there, a big movement toward urban renewal was going on,

In a corner of Eric Robertson's Peekskill living room, a simple office table and oak chairs pay homage to the painting by African-American artist Romare Bearden. The lamp is by African-American ceramicist Camille Billops.

which meant an enormous number of fine nineteenth-century buildings were being demolished to make way for new modern city projects. I began to pick up scraps of nineteenth-century buildings—moldings, statuary, glass —for almost nothing, ten dollars or so. I *loved* this stuff."

Eric moved to New York in 1968 and started working for hospitals and other institutions on issues of minority health rights, housing, and education. In 1970 he bought a house in Brooklyn, which he meticulously restored, incorporating some of the artifacts he had brought from his Chicago salvage trips, including two hundred pieces of leaded glass. Meanwhile, he became involved in an urban development corporation put together to help build communities with minority entrepreneurs. But still his other life preoccupied him. "Finally, I realized that what I really loved was art."

So he cut down on his legal work and devoted himself full-time to arts and crafts. He studied the great works of Charles Rennie Mackintosh, Antonio Gaudí, Frank Lloyd Wright. He started buying prints and ceramics, European Art Deco works that referred back to African, Egyptian, and non-Western forms. Gradually, perhaps inevitably, he was led to the art of his forebears, African art. "I was fascinated by this art," he says. "I didn't know it at all. With the rapid development of trade, business, and tourism between the African nations and the United States in the late sixties and early seventies,

suddenly African art was becoming known, and people were beginning to buy it with a passion."

In 1974 he opened the Grove Gallery in Greenwich Village, reflecting his newfound delight not only in African art but in contemporary crafts, in particular art jewelry. He soon became one of the foremost experts on African art and textiles. In 1980 he gave up his Grove Gallery to focus exclusively on the burgeoning interest in African art, and now has a large gallery in a loft on West Twenty-second Street filled with African antiquities, where he enthusiastically narrates the stories that lie behind each exotic mask and sculpture.

For someone who has led such a politically complex public life, Eric's private domain is surprisingly simple. He lives in a former slave's house in Peekskill, New York, overlooking a steep hillside. He gutted the interior, making brilliant use of the small space, preparatory to displaying a small but carefully chosen selection of his art. In fact it seems that the history of the house adds to the subtle impact of these dark, intricate pieces.

His taste is more eclectic now, and the house is like a geographical tour of African, Asian, and Caribbean nations. He has pieces from Ethiopia, Ghana, Zaire, Mexico, Haiti, Nigeria, Tanzania, the Caribbean, and China as well as furniture and art objects from Indonesia and the Philippines. "I see connections between cultures," he says. "Those connections inspire me."

TOP

On a shelf in the stairwell is a collection of Chinese Ming Dynasty heads, from a temple 1500 years old in Guangdong Province. Made of marble and gray stone, they are called "Blissful Buddhas."

ABOVE

In the bedroom, pillows from China and Ethiopia huddle cozily on top of a bedcover from central Africa. The bed is watched over by a collection of fertility dolls from Tanzania and other sculptures brought back from Africa.

RIGHT

Eric created this garden from a bare hillside, and enlivened it with some of his African art collection.

A New York loft is the perfect space to house Eric's huge collection of African, Caribbean, and American art, sculpture, furniture, religious objects, and textiles, along with an extensive art reference library.

PENNY & DAVID McCALL

THE HOUSE OF TWO PASSIONATE HUMANITARIANS

WHO ALSO LOVED ART.

David and Penny McCall started work four years ago on their Long Island house, which stands on the site of an old family home that belonged to Penny's great-great-grandfather, Edward Quimby, the first person to build a summer place in Bridgehampton. While each room in the house has its share of very personal art, the pictures on the walls are integrated with the color schemes and furnishings so smoothly that the overall experience is a luscious feast for the eye.

Strolling through the ground-floor rooms is like experiencing the evolution of art from the fifteenth through the twentieth century. Starting with the great room, a panegyric to the Italian Renaissance, we move through a sitting room reminiscent of an English country house library and through the master bedroom, a haven of sunlight and eclectic twentieth-century design. We finally end up in a long corridor that leads to the gallery where Penny's interest—avant-garde and conceptual work—pushes us firmly into the present.

Both Penny and David knew Italy very well, and the great room vividly reflects that knowledge. Their love of Italian art is everywhere in this glorious, glowing space,

from the Byzantine dome and the Giotto-like colors, to the Pompeii-inspired panels and moldings—all thanks to the brilliant brushwork of Rick Jordan, an architectural painter based in New York. "We worked from a palette of thirty colors," he explains, "and the finish was achieved with a mixture of plaster, sand, and paint."

The library is modeled on the English manner, with faux stucco walls, wood paneling, a library ladder, and well-stocked bookshelves. Penny acquired the seventeenth-century botanicals in England, and put them in storage, never imagining how well they would go together in this house. The pottery, discovered in Tuscany by the McCalls, is by Charles-Jean Avisseau, a ceramicist who revived the unusual art of the sixteenth-century potter Bernard Palissy. (Palissy's pitchers and vases with strange animal and plant designs, greatly admired by the Victorians, are mentioned in Anthony Trollope's *The Small House at Allington.*)

The bedroom is a light and sunny place, enhanced by the harlequin pattern painted—again by Rick Jordan—on the walls. "People are afraid of hanging pictures on top of finishes," Penny said. "I think they look great. Anyway, if you make a mistake, you can paint over it."

OPPOSITE

In the great room, a Bolivian headboard and photographs by Jonathan Becker are informally displayed on the mantel. Italian pottery decorates the shelves, in keeping with the Italianate theme of the room.

Also on the ground floor is a gallery where a selection of Penny's latest treasures can be seen—sculpture and conceptual art by American and international artists. It was on this very different planet, among the clustered wooden paddles, found art from Harlem, and mysterious Plexiglas boxes, that, artistically speaking, Penny was happiest.

"The first picture I bought was a Feliz Vercel painting," she remembers. "It's wonderfully awful—a poor man's impressionist. I still have it, just to remind myself. I have come a total 180 degrees in my art." Penny's great-aunt Catherine Ordway had a fine modern art collection—

Kiki Smith's fairies and an installation of scorched baseball bats by Jamaican artist Nari Ward dominates the corridor leading from the house to Penny McCall's gallery of conceptual art.

Calder, Giacometti, de Kooning—which she bequeathed to Yale University. Penny grew up absorbed by this art, and always loved pictures and objects, and putting them together. "I've always had an eye for interesting things—French pottery, Venetian glass, Italian ceramics. They are more decorative than fine art, but I see both as highly important. Crafts take as much talent as painting."

Her progress as an art lover took her from cozy, easy-to-live-with pictures and crafts to the farthest reaches of conceptualism. "I found I had this passion," she explained. "So I plunged in. I knew some artists and dealers, but really I needed direction." She met art adviser Carol Goldberg, who helped her find a more focused track. "We talk now as fellow collectors," Penny said. She concentrated on a small number of artists and had started a foundation to give grants to artists.

With suggestions from her husband, David McCall, whose eye was honed by working in advertising with such photographers as Irving Penn and Richard Avedon, the design of the Bridgehampton house was adapted to embrace Penny's aesthetic transformation. "When we were building the house we thought of adding a separate gallery to give us enough space to install some of these pieces. But David said plaintively, 'Can't we make it a *normal* house?' So we merged everything, and now we have 'normal' rooms with bookshelves and sofas and table lamps, and also a gallery."

The gallery is attached to the rest of the house by a corridor, which, while serving as display space for conceptual sculpture and art objects, also provides a transition from the safe and comfortable to the unsafe and uncomfortable. Penny knew. "Not everyone likes this art. If they are not interested, it's unfair to force it on them. As it is, the house can accommodate all tastes."

Today the house stands as a proud memorial to a couple whose commitment to human rights and the arts will never be forgotten.

LEFT

The harlequin pattern on the bedroom walls makes a hospitable background for the art. The stacked photographs by conceptual artists in the corridor are frequently moved around by Penny.

BELOW

In the library, the set of twelve English botanical engravings over the sofa offer a pleasing interplay with the shelves of books. The round Avisseau plates break up the rectangular hang.

Davidson's Hudson Valley dining room is a studied mix of art and
furniture periods. Bruno Fonseca's contemporary abstract cityscape is
positioned above an antique Chinese altar chest. A stark Lynn Davis
photograph of Niagara Falls looks down on an English Regency dining
table and a turn-of-the-century decoy from Maryland.

JOAN K. DAVIDSON

IN THE COMPANY OF NEW NEIGHBORS A WORK OF ART TAKES ON A WHOLE NEW CHARACTER — AND THE ROOM CHANGES TOO.

"Works of art must fit into the total canvas," Joan Davidson says, "in harmony with all the other elements." As they do in both her Manhattan apartment where there is no room to spare and in her sprawling Hudson River historic house, Midwood, where she has "lovely acres of waste space." She explains, "I see a work of art in relationship to the floor, ceiling, architecture, view outside, color palette, quality of light, furniture, even plant life. Each aspect contributes to a satisfying whole, especially if there is a paring-down that results in a minimum of extraneous stuff."

In both homes, Davidson has meticulously arranged and integrated the art and furniture she inherited from her mother, Alice M. Kaplan, and the beautiful things she continues to search for. Of her mother, Joan says, "She loved antiquities and art of all times and cultures. My mother's design sense was instinctual and stayed with her." Davidson recalls that even when her mother suffered from Alzheimer's, "she would sit at the table and make patterns with the spoons and any other objects in front of her."

For seventeen years Davidson was president of the J. M. Kaplan Fund in New York, founded by her father to support the arts, parks, conservation, human rights, and projects benefiting New York City and State. In 1993 she left the fund to become New York State commissioner of parks, recreation and historic preservation.

Three years later Joan became an executor of her mother's collection of old master drawings, American folk art, pre-Columbian art, Asian sculpture, and contemporary paintings, which had been bequeathed to museums as well as to Joan and her siblings, who took turns choosing the art and furniture they wanted. "It was interesting to discover that mostly we were devoted to different things," she says.

Davidson chose paintings by Blakelock, Vuillard, and Brewster and drawings by Tiepolo, Daumier, Guardi, and Kensett. She also cherishes several sculptural works that luck-of-the-draw brought to her, notably a stone sculpture by Gonzalo Fonseca, her former brother-in-law. She talks enthusiastically about her mother's heroic bronze Nadelman, which she took up to her country house and exchanged with a poetic Mary Frank sculpture she bought herself. "I thought it would look better in my city apartment because it shares the same romantic feeling as the Blakelock and the solitude of the Vuillard. It also adds warm terra-cotta color to the living room and softens the architectural line of the bookcases behind it."

Davidson enjoys moving objects back and forth between her city and upstate homes. "When you move things," she observes, "you see the art afresh, in different space and light. In the company of new neighbors a work of art takes on a whole new character—and the room changes too." And she admits to having an idiosyncratic point of view about lighting art. "Little spots of light wash out the color in a painting," she feels. "Table lamps are warm and welcoming, but too many of them make me dizzy. I admire a room that has one or two strong decisive lamps in a setting where general illumination comes from subtle sources, like uplights and picture lights or even candlelight. And you can't improve on those always marvelous Noguchi lamps that are artworks in themselves."

Davidson's homes mirror each other in their engaging mix of old and new art. She admits to "not sticking to the rules." In Manhattan she surrounded an eighteenth-

century Italian gilded console with 1920s French leather chairs and topped it off with her turn-of-the-century Vuillard drawing. In her Hudson Valley home, Davidson hung eighteenth-century French etchings in the drawing room on frescoed walls inspired by the Pompeii rooms at the Metropolitan Museum. Painted by a local artist, they were commissioned to capture Hudson Valley's bird life, side by side with birds of antiquity. A starkly modern Lynn Davis black-and-white photograph of Niagara Falls dominates the dining room, in counterpoint to a sophisticated antique Chinese altar chest.

Textiles and rugs add warmth, beauty, and storytelling enchantment to Davidson's homes. The black-and-silver shawl she framed in the bedroom of her apartment was a gift from her friend and former teacher Martha Graham. "She wore it in the 1929 Follies," Joan reveals. The dramatic Fortuny cut-velvet opera coat she found at the New York Winter Antiques Sale was framed and hung in the living room of her city apartment. "Merely moving it to another wall somehow defined a new place for sitting and talking." At Midwood, a fifteenth-century Peruvian textile hangs from the ceiling, protected by glass, welcoming you to the sleeping quarters of the house, where rugs are hung as headboards in several of the bedrooms. In the living room, rugs are layered as a protective ploy, since "the best one in the house," her mother's ancient Spanish Cuenca, is badly worn.

ABOVE

On the fireplace wall in Davidson's New York living room is a portrait by John Brewster, Jr., and a G. D. Tiepolo drawing above an eighteenth-century Italian chest. A framed Fortuny cut-velvet opera coat hangs above the couch. Stacks of art books surround an African basket on an antique English library table.

RIGHT

Joan, her daughter, Betsy, and granddaughter, Phoebe, sit in front of a landscape she inherited from her mother, Blakelock's Moonlight. *"At first I had drawings on either side of it," Joan says, "but then I decided it could hold the wall by itself."*

Davidson commissioned a local artist to paint Hudson Valley birdlife on the walls of her double parlor. Romanticized portraits of each of her four children dominate rooms with backlit walls of books, reading room furniture, and a still life of her grandchildren's toys.

Davidson explains the seasoned, time-worn look that personalizes her houses as fulfilling an aesthetic principle she adheres to rigorously. "Nothing in nature is spanking new all the time: renewal and decay are always side by side and are equally necessary," she says. "That's my justification for changing things all the time but letting my fraying furniture be; it's the natural way. Art shines in these surroundings."

INSIGHT, PERSISTENCE & DARING

THE DOROTHY & HERBERT VOGEL STORY

In the smallest of bedrooms, the Vogels make space for an Allen Saret sculpture (on the dresser), too fragile to transport to the National Gallery, and recent acquisitions—two Michael Lucero ceramics, a Cheryl Laemmle canvas, and three Richard Tuttle sculptures.

Their home, a one-bedroom apartment in a nondescript New York high-rise, would not qualify for *House Beautiful,* but it is a mecca for artists, curators, collectors, and cognoscenti of the international art world.

Dorothy and Herbert Vogel's story is now legend. A postal worker and a librarian, they devoted one-half of their annual income, during thirty years of marriage, to the creation of a collection of late-twentieth-century minimalist and conceptual art. Then, in 1992, they pledged two thousand works by two hundred artists

from the 1960s through the 1990s to the National Gallery of Art. And immediately started all over again.

"The Vogels were on my radar screen in the early seventies," recalls Jack Cowart, the man responsible for bringing the Vogel collection to the National. Now deputy director of the Corcoran Gallery of Art, Cowart explains that the Vogels were "determined to educate people to art that many considered obscure and esoteric. Herb's moral compass was clear."

Cowart's first visit to the Vogel apartment was daunting. "There was this mountain of wrapped art," he said. "Crates on top of crates on top of boxes." They logged things mentally, never keeping a full inventory because they would have had to move out of their 'fortress of art' to do it. Their apartment was so crammed that they stored seventy Richard Tuttle artworks under their bed. Despite Dorothy's library skills and archival dedication, Herb would stick things into folders, milk crates, and shoe boxes, which were under chairs or buried in the back of closets." Reduced to 15 square feet of living space, they had just enough room for a kitchen table, three chairs, their pet turtles, an aquarium, and five cats named Corot, Picasso, Degas, Cézanne, and Manet. The art the Vogels hung sporadically on their walls was covered with remnants of fabric to shield it from light and view. "You had these tantalizing glimpses of things," Cowart says. "You could feel the collection, but you couldn't see it. . . .

"There were many scary moments when Herb would call and say, 'Remember that two-inch rope? Well, it's a very important Tuttle work, so tell me when you find it.' Then there was the Robert Lobe piece that was missing for months until we realized it was stuck between two pieces of cardboard that we mistook for an empty envelope."

In the fall and winter of 1990, four truckloads of art were moved from the Vogels' small apartment to the museum, where the painstaking process of inventorying thousands of disparate works began. They filled a major gap in the museum's holdings. A barrage of media attention followed the acceptance by the museum of the drawings, paintings, and sculpture the Vogels had assembled "with insight, persistence and daring," as described in the catalog the National Gallery published for its fiftieth anniversary exhibition, *Works from the Dorothy and Herbert Vogel Collection.*

Asked why they chose the National Gallery over the many other art institutions vying for their collection, the Vogels replied, "It's the people's museum, no entry fees are charged, and it doesn't sell anything it accepts. We worked for the government all our lives and it was our way of paying back." As an afterthought Herb says, "We spent our honeymoon in Washington, and Dorothy got her first art lesson when I took her to the National Gallery."

When Herb was in his late twenties and working at the post office, he was also studying art history at New York University and the Institute of Fine Arts, prowling the museums and galleries and "hanging out" with artists at the Cedar Bar. Vogel says, "They were inventing art that everyone was saying wasn't art. They were stimulating and different. I listened and learned a lot."

After they married, Herb and Dorothy spent weekends visiting artists in their studios. "We were able to buy art that few understood or wanted at very low prices. The first piece we bought together was a John Chamberlain sculpture. But the turning point for me," Herb reveals, "was meeting Sol LeWitt in 1965. I had long talks with him about art, and I was the first to buy his work. Bob Mangold helped him bring the piece to our apartment and hang it. The art world was small then; everybody knew each other and helped each other."

"What drove us in the beginning, drives us still," Dorothy explains. "We're interested in the artists' evolution. LeWitt has become more painterly. Tuttle is using different materials. Christo and Jeanne-Claude are mapping *The Gates in Central Park,* we'll follow that project as we did when they surrounded the islands in Miami and wrapped the Reichstag in Berlin. Their new work will add depth to our collection."

THE ARTISTS' VIEW OF THE VOGELS

Package *(1974), by Christo*

Christo & Jeanne-Claude

Engraved in our minds is the time the Vogels called to say they wanted to visit our studio. It was 1970 and we had recently arrived in New York from Paris. We assumed they were wealthy because they were listed in the art magazines as major collectors. We looked at each other and thought, Now we'll be able to pay the rent.

Later, when we visited them and saw how they loved their cats, we proposed an exchange. We would give them a collage of the valley curtain project we were working on in Colorado if they would keep our cat, Gladys, while we were away. They did!

The art the Vogels collect is a difficult art; their fidelity, passion, and intelligence made it possible. They spent a week following us on our *Running Fence* project in northern California and documented it with photographs. Dorothy told everyone that *Running Fence* was an important part of the Vogel collection. She was right, because *Running Fence* belongs to the fifty-nine ranchers on whose land it was built and to all those who came to experience and live it as the Vogels did.

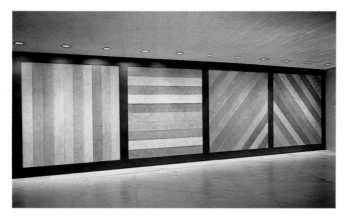

Wall Drawing No. 681 C, *by Sol LeWitt installed in the National Gallery in 1993.*

Sol LeWitt

I was thirty when I first met Herb Vogel at the Cedar Bar. There'd be bar talk, art talk, and real estate talk—artists mostly talk about where to find a place to live and work.

I had a studio on West Broadway, and Herb came down to see my stuff. Sometime later he brought Dorothy. She was very sharp, knowledgeable, and rational. Herb was more emotional. But they always chose together.

When I had my first show, in 1967, Herb bought the only piece I sold, so my estimation of him improved a lot. Then I decided I didn't like it and gave him another piece in exchange because I wanted to destroy it. Vogel says that if I asked to do that today, he would never give it back.

They didn't pursue grand art with great names. The Vogels are the guardians of a period of art that would have been lost if they hadn't had the obsessive drive to understand and collect it. By perpetuating art, they perpetuated themselves. Because Herb was there from the very beginning, I make art I'm doing now accessible to them.

Robert & Sylvia Mangold

You always think of them as Herb and Dorothy; they are equal partners in what they do. They go to everything and are seen at all the openings. In 1965 they came to our studio and our first apartment on the Lower East Side. They were unknown and so were we. They quickly became supporters of our work and would pay whatever they could afford, which was helpful. The first work of mine they bought was *3½ Circles,* and we're not sure if they paid for it at once or over time. The Vogels never thought in terms of money. Even when artists they collected became famous, Herb and Dorothy would not sell their works.

There is no other like Herb Vogel. He'll walk around your studio and pick out the best work you're doing every time. Dorothy will discover another piece and they'll talk about it. Then they'll say, "What do you think?" We'll go back and forth like this for a long time because Herb enjoys talking about art as much as looking at it.

ABOVE, LEFT

Red/Green X Within X *(1981), by Robert Mangold*

ABOVE, RIGHT

Studio Corner in the Morning with Window Light Across the Floor *(1972), by Sylvia Plimack Mangold*

Primal Energy III (Earth Sounds) *(1989), by Edda Renouf*

Edda Renouf

I was always fascinated with the way the Vogels lived.
Their home was a work of art itself, as original as they
are. They are the mystery even as art is mysterious.

Showing them my art was always uplifting. They
would come over regularly to see my series of drawings
when I lived in New York; they have 110 works of mine.
Now that I'm in Paris, they write regularly to communicate their enthusiasm for the new work I'm doing.
Only last year they bought one of my pieces that was
considered too new and outrageous for collectors.
The Vogels took it to the National Gallery and said it
belonged in their collection. When you feel like a loner
and no one can relate to what you're doing, the Vogels
affirm your vision and others begin to see. They've
made it their profession to spread the word about art
that wasn't acknowledged until recently. Young people
should be as brave as they were.

Richard Tuttle

I've always seen the Vogels' apartment as a metaphor
for the dead letter department of the post office Herb
worked in for thirty-two years. Early on, he was interested in art that was "undeliverable." All artists make art
in the sense that you might post a letter. If it's fashion-
able, it gets delivered. If it's not, it doesn't. The brilliance
of the Vogels' collection is this sympathy for work that
was undeliverable.

The Vogels first saw my work when my *Cloth
Octagonals* was on exhibit in 1968. Herb and Dorothy
were enthusiastic but couldn't afford it at the time.
But at my fourth show, they paid a hundred dollars for
a large multiple, saying it was a mistake to have passed
up my earlier work. I installed it for them myself.

Right from the start, our relationship was about art.
Herb's a schmoozer. We would spend nights talking until
four in the morning, about my work and what others
were doing. We dreamed of their collection finding
a museum and then it happened, but it didn't end there.
The Vogels are still acquiring works by artists they've
followed from the beginning.

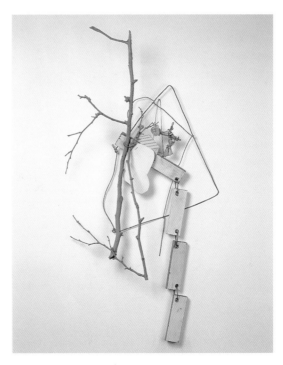

Monkey's Recovery for a Darkened Room (Bluebird) *(1983),
by Richard Tuttle*

IN AN ARTIST'S STUDIO

CHRISTINA ROSSETTI

One face looks out from all his canvases,

One selfsame figure sits or walks or leans;

We found her hidden just behind those screens,

That mirror gave back all her loveliness.

A queen in opal or in ruby dress,

A nameless girl in freshest summer-greens,

A saint, an angel;--every canvass means

The same one meaning, neither more nor less.

He feeds upon her face by day and night,

And she with true kind eyes looks back on him

Fair as the moon and joyful as the light:

Not wan with waiting, not with sorrow dim;

Not as she is, but was when hope shone bright;

Not as she is, but as she fills his dreams.

ARTISTS AT HOME

DON BACHARDY

FOR DON WITH LOVE.

HAPPY BIRTHDAY, CHRIS.

If a man is blessed with a talent for friendship, one of the most pleasing ways of displaying this talent is on the walls of his house. Such a man is Don Bachardy, portrait artist, whose longtime companionship with Christopher Isherwood, author of *Prater Violet, A Single Man, Goodbye to Berlin* (which inspired the musical *Cabaret*), and other stories and plays, was one of the great alliances of the twentieth century. The house they shared is still filled with visual mementos of their extraordinary friendship.

They met when Don Bachardy was eighteen and Christopher Isherwood was forty-eight, and they lived together until Isherwood's death in 1986. Bachardy was only a fledgling painter when he set up house with Isherwood in 1953. "In my early childhood I was already drawing," Bachardy recalls, "and even then all my pictures were of people." But his father was opposed to his son's artistic career and actively tried to stop it. Isherwood's encouragement was vital at that time. "I'd have never been a painter without Chris," Bachardy says. It was Christopher who encouraged him to concentrate on portraits, a visual form of Isherwood's diary. Thus the painter started recording in paint, just as the writer recorded in words,

and they began their journey through life together expressing their experiences in their art.

Don's first portraits were of his artist friends, and if they liked the painting, they traded for it. "Having an artist as a sitter," Bachardy says, "brings something special to the portrait and makes one know more about the artist." His first portraits were in pencil, and then for many years he worked only in pen and ink. As he grew more confident, he moved into color. His subjects, from Fred Astaire to Robert Mapplethorpe, are from all walks of life and include both the famous and the unknown.

Bachardy and Isherwood moved into this house in Santa Monica in 1959. Originally Don used the garage as a studio, but later they added a second floor to the garage to create a bigger, lighter space for his studio. It is filled with Bachardy's dramatic, vivid portraits. Inside the house, the feeling is peaceful and calm. Most of the walls are white, which Bachardy believes is the best background for the pictures. "Once I painted the bedroom scarlet and hung denim curtains, but soon changed it back to white." Indeed, many of the pictures Bachardy and Isherwood purchased or were given over the years are delicate watercolors, which would be overwhelmed by deeply colored

OPPOSITE

Around the hearth, artist friends of Don and Christopher have left their mark. Over the mantel is a still life by Paul Wonner.

OVERLEAF

The mirrored wall at the far end of the dining area reflects the walls of the sunken living room, creating the effect of a double-length gallery of art.

Don Bachardy in his studio, surrounded by his raw and powerful late portraits of Christopher Isherwood. He always works from life, and completes the painting in one sitting. "A sitting is a true collaboration," he says.

In Christopher's study, above the daybed is a portrait of Don and Chris by David Hockney. The drawing, inscribed "Happy Birthday Chris," is by Paul Wonner. The watercolors are by Christopher's father.

walls. The California light (mostly indirect sunlight since the house is tucked into the side of a hill) is itself enough to enhance the subtle palettes.

Every part of the house speaks of these two men's friendship not only with each other but with the artistic and literary world they inhabited for over thirty years. Don and Christopher presided over a kind of southern Californian salon for philosophers, writers, and seekers after truth. While Don painted (always from life), Isherwood wrote and pursued his interest in mysticism and Eastern religions. The house was always filled with European émigrés eager to discuss politics, movies, art, and spiritual matters ranging from Zen Buddhism to the Bhagavad Gita, ideas that were to appear later in Isherwood's diaries and memoirs.

Although Isherwood has been dead for over ten years, his spirit is everywhere, not only in the writer's study, which looks almost as if he had left the typewriter only a moment ago, but also on the walls of the house, where so many of the pictures are dedicated to Don and Chris. "For Don with love. Happy birthday, Chris." "Special proof for Christopher and Don with much love from David Hockney, 1977." Such personal messages are everywhere. Hockney, Patrick Procktor, Paul Wonner, and Ed Ruscha are just some of the artists who expressed their appreciation with a painting after visiting this artists' haven, flooded with light, hospitality, and intellectual stimuli. "After a while we ran out of wall space," Bachardy admits.

Don and Chris also gave strong encouragement to young artists, whose work they bought. As Don says, "Moral support to keep going is very important when you are young." Bachardy believes that commitment to art is more than just a talent for painting. "I think that drive is at least as important as talent, if not more so," he says.

Bachardy is still fueled by this drive, and friends continue to visit. But while their presence still lingers wherever one looks, perhaps the most powerful tribute to this unique couple lies in the series of paintings and sketches

The light-filled living room, with a view overlooking the garden,
is a showcase for artists, including the work of Michael Davis,
Ed Ruscha, and Karen Carson (on the ceiling beam) and sculpture
in the foreground by Phyllis Green and Joe Fay.

Don did during the last six months of Christopher's life. During that time, Christopher was Don's only subject, and that daily intensity between artist and sitter brought them to an almost total communion of souls. "The gaze that meets . . . the eye of the painter is one of self-knowledge dearly bought," wrote Christopher Hitchens about these works of Bachardy's. The paintings comfort Bachardy, now that Isherwood is no longer here to sit for him. Meanwhile, he paints, working, in the words of a Vedantic teaching, "for the work itself, not the fruits thereof."

JENNIFER BARTLETT

I LIKE LOOKING AT THESE PAINTINGS EVERY DAY —
NOT JUST MINE BUT OTHER PEOPLE'S.

L iving well is the best revenge" springs to mind when Jennifer Bartlett explains her motivation for creating one of her most ambitious artworks—her home. "I was determined to discover whether my ideas for the Battery Park City garden project, scuttled after six years of effort, would work," Jennifer explains. "It became an obsession. I decided to look for a place where I could build a garden, and that's how it all started."

Bartlett acted as her own architect. She transformed an industrial building, an anachronism at the end of one of the most romantic streets in Greenwich Village, into a country house in the city: "I planned an environment that would give me everything I like in my life, starting with a lot of great space—green space and wall space." You are not as aware of intimate living space as you are of space given over to her paintings and her garden. Two floors of the four-story house are devoted to her studio. A garden that runs the full width of the house is framed by two massive glass doors, providing the illusion of landscape murals in her living room. Conceived to be a multi-experience, all-seasons garden, it rises up three levels to a top-floor indoor pool. All the elements that

are important to Bartlett and are reflected in her art are here—earth, water, light, space.

Bartlett's home comes close to being her autobiography. Wall-to-wall and floor-to-ceiling art is arranged from one end of the house to the other, providing a retrospective of her own work and a view of the artists she admires. "It's nice to see my own work in relationship

ABOVE

In a room big enough to be a factory with rolling wagons filled with paints and brushes, Bartlett mounts a scaffold to work on a piece from her 1997 Water *series.*

OPPOSITE

Echoing the stairs that lead from Bartlett's studio to her living space is a staircase chest she found at a Kyoto flea market while researching her design for a temple ceiling. Bartlett's paintings commandeer the walls.

OVERLEAF

Bartlett's combination sculpture/painting, Boats and Houses, *dominates one end of her living room. Peter Schlesinger's yellow pot ornaments the pass-through counter to the kitchen.*

to that of others," she says. "Wherever I've lived, I've wanted to be surrounded by the art of my friends. I have four Elizabeth Murrays. We met in college and have been close ever since. Two very different pieces of hers are in my living room, along with an oil sketch I bought from Alex Katz, who did a portrait of my friends and me in my old house." Bartlett points out other works she enjoys because they are "just so beautiful"; the work of former assistants.

"I never used to surround myself with my work," Jennifer says. "But now that I am not represented by a primary dealer, I store all my own stuff. I thought, Why not have my paintings out so I can look at them and think about them. I keep finding new spaces to hang things. I'll start out making one kind of change and end up making another. Sometimes things go out for shows, so I replace them. I don't think a lot of people would hang a seven-foot, three-dimensional painting in a three-foot viewing space," Bartlett says, referring to the paintings from her Fire series in the hallway. "But it doesn't bother me. This is where I live, and I can do what I want."

Bartlett lines two parallel hallways with a grid of ceiling-to-floor paintings. Leading into the living room are studies for her Japanese temple ceiling, rich in water, nature, and animal imagery.

Nothing in her house upstages the art. The furniture in her living room, library, and bedroom is unpretentious. "An interior designer would look with horror at what I have around," Jennifer admits laughingly. "When Marian McEvoy, the editor of *Elle Decor,* was redoing her house, I traded one of my plate pieces for her rugs. A weird couch with leather straps in my library was my first furniture purchase. I bought it at a fire sale, and it's literally charred. I just re-cover it every so often because I think there is heart in an old sofa. A Japanese friend made my living room table twenty-five years ago, and I bought reproductions of Hoffmann chairs to go with it. Acquiring a new piece of furniture is always a radical move for me, so I haven't bought anything new in years."

Bartlett's spartan bedroom is warmed by some very personal art pieces arranged along the edge of the ceiling so that she can see them when she lies in bed. She is surrounded by a watercolor by Madison Cox, the landscape architect who collaborated with her on her garden and Battery Park project, and works by artist Joel Shapiro and photographer Eric Boman. Reminiscent of her days at

By the window in her daughter's room hangs a painting by Jan Hashey above a work that Jasper Johns gave Bartlett when Alice was born.

Yale is a painting by former art department chairman Jack Tworkov. Most amusing of all is one half of a drawing by Jonathan Borofsky, her Yale classmate and longtime friend. He gave the other half to Paula Cooper, since Jennifer and her former dealer share the same birthday.

Jennifer painted the glass doors leading into her bedroom from the living room with plaited ribbons of color to form a plaid grid that gives her sleeping space both light and privacy. Her love of plaids, which she describes as "a human kind of grid," can be seen in nearly everything she does, from the grid structure in her enamel plate pieces to the organization of her compartmentalized garden.

It is perhaps this tangle of interconnections between life and art that make Bartlett one of the most inventive of contemporary artists. "Everything is either a work she has created, figures in her work, or influences her work in one

form or another," Madison Cox explains. There is ample evidence of this throughout Bartlett's home. At the top of the stairwell that leads into her living space is a *kaidan-dansu,* a wooden staircase chest that Bartlett found in a Kyoto flea market while searching for Japanese objects to incorporate into her design for a temple ceiling. She filled the drawers with these objects and brought it all home. The walls of her laundry room are lined with display boxes of mounted butterflies that appear in her Fire series, one of which hangs over the fireplace in her library.

Asked how she decides which of her artworks to live with, Bartlett answers, "Sometimes I just pick one to keep. A lot of times my favorites are the least popular ones in the show. So it's what I want, and it's also what I end up with."

Display boxes of butterflies that figure in works from Bartlett's Fire series line the walls of the laundry room.

JON HENDRICKS

INTIMACY WITH THE WORK IS ESSENTIAL, TO HAVE IT AROUND YOU, TO RESPOND TO AT DIFFERENT TIMES.

Most dogs sit when you say "Sit." Jon Hendricks's dog sits when you say "Marcel Duchamp." A Dada dog in the home of this curator, collector, and artist is only to be expected. Jon Hendricks first studied to be an artist. "My work was action-oriented," he said. "In the 1960s we wanted to communicate what was happening within that very moment, to encapsulate the ephemeral."

This is how Hendricks came to Fluxus, an international art movement that emerged in the 1960s in reaction to the personality cultism and commercialization of art. "'Fluxus' means change, flowing, also something you put into something else to make it harder," explains Hendricks, who is now curator of the Gilbert and Lila Silverman Fluxus Collection in Detroit, Michigan, as well as organizing exhibitions of Yoko Ono's work. "'Fluxus' also means purging. So you see, it's a very powerful concept!"

The roots of Fluxus lie in Dada, and Hendricks has a splendid collection of Dadaist posters and pictures. But Fluxus art is his specialty, and as curator to the Silvermans, he is in charge of one of the foremost Fluxus art collections in the world.

Yet he and his family live and work, not in some avant-garde white cube, but in a Greenwich Village house that dates from 1810 and contains echoes of America's architectural past. One might question this collision of old and new, but Hendricks sees no conflict. To him, a house is a growing thing. "The art you live with is what you feel stimulated by and comfortable with. I feel the same way about this house. There is never just one period that has to be frozen in time. We like to mix Pennsylvania Dutch furniture with the most modern Japanese artwork. Thus each room becomes constantly exciting."

"Art should be in a home," he says. "Intimacy with the work is essential, to have it around you, to rediscover at different times. That way you keep it alive. When you live with an object it is like a book. You might not use it—then one day you'll delve into it and discover something of its mystery. With your art, you should smile when you see it, respond emotionally to it. Once it is in a museum, that feeling is killed. That personal contact is gone."

OPPOSITE, TOP

Eleonore Hendricks's room is full of youthful visual stimuli, including an early Al Hansen work that she bought herself.

OPPOSITE, BOTTOM

In the living room, many of Jon Hendricks's passions are on display: candle piece by Nam Jun Paik, hands by Jim Dine, armor by Roy Lichtenstein, Ray Gun by Claes Oldenburg, caged objects by Tetsumi Kudo, baking pan with sausages by Yayoi Kusama.

CYNTHIA HAZEN POLSKY

WE ARE SURROUNDED BY SO MUCH INDIAN CULTURE — FOOD, MUSIC, LITERATURE, AND ART — THAT INDIA SEEMS ALMOST LIKE OLD HOME COUNTRY TO OUR FAMILY.

A sixty-second elevator ride up to Cynthia and Leon Polsky's sky-high apartment in Manhattan is like a trip on a magic carpet. Cross the threshold and you are in a sitting room that could be the set for a Merchant-Ivory film—richly ornamented with sensually upholstered furniture, antique Indian wall hangings, and exotic objects. A nineteenth-century replica of one of the great Mughal rugs from India's Golden Age and the sound of a cooing dove add to the romantic fantasy.

"India is a cornucopia of creative life. I am moved by the intimate relationship that exists between various arts in Indian culture," the painter Cynthia Polsky explains as she talks about their collection of sixteenth- to nineteenth-century Indian paintings. "We live with and enjoy these paintings and many of the textiles and objects we've collected that appear in them. We are surrounded by so much Indian culture—food, music, literature, and art—that India seems almost like old home country to our family. Our sons, who grew up with Indian paintings, myths, and legends, think of Indian food as soul food.

ABOVE

In the bedroom, the Polskys hung a radiant festival banner from an Indian temple, depicting the divine couple, Radha and Krishna. Fanned open, the peacocks' tails signify that they have made love.

OPPOSITE

Cynthia created her fantasy sitting room with saffron walls, lush fabric hangings, and a great Mughal rug. Centered in the room is a nineteenth-century Damaskas table inlaid with ivory, ebony, and mother of pearl. An eighteenth-century image of milkmaids presenting offerings to Krishna dominates the far wall.

"Many of the paintings are a narration of the life cycle," Cynthia continues. "It's an emotive kind of art—positive, uplifting, rich in imagery, and intellectually challenging. There is also a practical aspect to living with Indian art," she tells you. "Because much of Indian art is small, you can contain a comprehensive collection in an apartment."

Because their paintings are easy to handle and arrange, the Polskys change them frequently. "It also gives us the opportunity to look at those we have stored away," Cynthia says, describing the Indian custom of wrapping paintings in cloth or clothes before sheltering them in drawers and closets. They can then be taken out, unwrapped, and held like a book. "Sometimes we listen to Indian music when we look at them. These fragile paintings were never meant to be hung. They were meant to be seen the way music is meant to be heard, intimately. Indian cultural activities were enjoyed in tandem. There is even a school of painting called ragamala, which relates to the Indian musical tradition and interprets its poetic symbolism.

"I fell in love with Indian things when I was nine years old," Cynthia remembers. "I was in bed with a cold one day and opened a book called *Made in India*. I can still see the photograph of two women in saris drifting across fertile plains with brass containers on their heads. I knew then that this was a place I would have to make part of my life. My father, Joseph Hazen, thought it was odd that I would focus on this remote place when there was so much art to discover closer in time and spirit. He was a passionate collector of contemporary Western art. I remember a girl in my class giving me a quarter to see the double-headed Picasso hanging over our fireplace."

Fortunately, Cynthia's husband, Leon, a lawyer, shares her love of adventurous travel and art. They took their first trip abroad in 1960 and spent several months discovering Asia and the Middle East, including India. "We have collected Indian pictures in a serious way for more than thirty years," Cynthia says. "I've also searched

for objects and textiles similar to those that appear in these paintings."

Cynthia has definite ideas about how Indian art should be seen, arranged, and preserved. "It's a challenge to create a healthy home for art and still make it aesthetically pleasing," Cynthia says. "When we made our corridor into a gallery, we accomplished two things: people could view the art at close range, and it precluded the need for strong direct light." Because Indian paintings are densely peopled and detailed, "They don't do well in a cluttered arrangement or room setting; they require ample surrounding space."

Art that Cynthia inherited from her parents, Joseph and Lita Annenberg Hazen, early collectors of modern masterworks, adds an element of surprise to the living room. A Léger painting and a Giacometti sculpture coexist with the nineteenth- and early-twentieth-century silver and porcelain they prize and enjoy using. Cynthia's expressionist paintings are equally serendipitous, forming a harmonic transition between the modern and Indian collections. "We are accustomed to seeing twentieth-century art together with African art but not with the cultures of India and southeast Asia. I was excited to find that my paintings worked so well with Indian art. I discovered that contemporary art doesn't have to be segregated. It can be integrated into an environment that is more decorative and colorful."

OPPOSITE, TOP

A framed sixteenth-century Turkish Ottoman cover of silk and velvet is braced by two Cynthia Polsky canvases (1973)—a sensual backdrop for eighteenth-century British campaign chairs and cane furniture covered in Indian fabrics.

OPPOSITE, BOTTOM

In the Polsky dining room, seventeenth- and eighteenth-century Indian watercolors bracket the Léger masterwork Cynthia inherited. An eclectic group of art objects is displayed on Anne Sperry's dragon-tooth serving table, made of salvaged materials.

102

COSTANTINO & RUTH NIVOLA

LIFE AND ART WERE NOT SEPARATE.

FOR US, IT WAS ONE THING.

Step over the sand-cast sculpture that lies like a welcome mat at the front door of Ruth Nivola's 1754 farmhouse on eastern Long Island, and you walk into one of Costantino Nivola's color-saturated artworks. You become a figure in the three-dimensional still life that Ruth's late husband created when they moved into their story-book house fifty years ago. Tino, as everyone called him, painted the wooden floors mercury yellow in the kitchen–dining room and narrow staircase that leads up to the bedrooms. "It brought sunshine into our home on gloomy days," Ruth says.

"To make room for living and the art that was our life," Ruth explains, "Tino broke down room-dividing walls. He created space for his paintings and sculpture, the art my parents rescued when they fled Nazi Europe, my daughter Claire's art, and the work of several of Tino's friends—Josef Albers, Saul Steinberg, Hedda Sterne, and Le Corbusier. Corbu," she remembers, "visited us soon after we bought the farmhouse and saw adjoining empty walls as an invitation to paint two floor-to-ceiling abstract murals." A seating arrangement on the floor of cushions that Le Corbusier insisted upon and the Indian prayer rug that Ruth's father gave her provide the perfect setting for contemplation of these witty, colorful paintings and an iconic wood sculpture from Tino's Great Mother series.

The palette and placement of each element in the Nivola home were carefully considered to satisfy Tino's personal aesthetic and to enlarge and enliven the dark, cloistered rooms of their eighteenth-century farmhouse. "To Tino, the visual was everything," Ruth says, explaining her husband's intense concern for every aspect of their surroundings. "When Tino went to a hotel, even for only one night, he would take down the paintings, hide them in the closet, and rearrange all the furniture. He couldn't exist for a moment in a room that was ugly or disharmonious. . . . Life and art were not separate. For us, it was one thing."

Ruth met Tino in Italy when they were both in art school, and from the very beginning she shared his desire for simplicity. "When you're poor," she observed, "that's how you live rich." Their son, Pietro, echoes her

OPPOSITE

Longtime friend, Le Corbusier, painted the murals on adjoining walls, observing that the low ceilings were perfectly proportioned for the Nivolas since they were very short people.

OVERLEAF

To open up 10-foot ceilings, Tino Nivola painted them watercolor blue and hung three handcrafted Sardinian baskets high on the wall. He painted a rocking chair stoke-fire red to contrast with the woodburning stove that stands like sculpture in the center of the room. Le Corbusier's mural can be seen through the doorway.

108

"The whole house is my skin," Ruth says. "Tino placed things so well, I keep everything the way he left it." A Tino collage complements his bronzes on a low bookcase along with his sculpture of a pregnant Ruth, and a terra cotta head by daughter, Claire.

sentiment when he says, "Even when we were living on a shoestring, we were always surrounded by art, which was much more uplifting than the luxuries money would bring." Ruth attributes Tino's purist approach to the fact that he grew up in "an old Italian peasant house that had no furniture, no decoration, and no art on the walls. He was critical of the overdecorated, bourgeois home that I came from."

The Nivola sensibility also extends to the 34 acres of land that surround the house. Tino transformed a rich portion of this vast greenscape into a field of art with graphic murals painted on cinder-block walls to create

islands of beauty with stone sculptures nestled among shrubs and beds of lilies of the valley and a sculptured dome-shaped oven where Tino baked bread and pizza.

When Tino first saw the tall cedars that border this rolling green lawn, he was reminded of his Mediterranean roots. He was impressed by the special quality of light which also attracted his artist neighbors, the abstract expressionists who joined him in creating a congenial artists' community on Long Island. Its landscapes and seascapes called up childhood memories of watching his stonemason father at work and provided Tino with the inspiration for his great sand-cast reliefs, which incorporated the texture and quality of the shore. Sand-casting is a technique he developed while playing with his children on a nearby beach, making relief sculptures by pouring cement into molded sand. Le Corbusier joined him one day, Ruth recalls, and "Corbu became very excited about this new method and asked Tino to teach him how to do it." One of the painted pieces that Le Corbusier made hangs in the entry hall of the Nivola home.

With his new casting technique, Tino moved from painting to sculpture. In the 1950s, his career as a sculptor for architectural and public art projects took off, and models for his many commissions from universities and international corporations remain in the studio that he built across the lawn. Ruth has preserved intact not only their home but also the working environment that shaped her husband's career.

"Time stopped for my mother when my father died," Pietro says. "Although he used to change things constantly, my mother insists that everything stay put, the way my father left them." His sister, Claire, remembers "paintings on the wall that you'd look at while lying in bed. Growing up the way I did, art wasn't some precious thing. It was just something someone made and loved."

The art of friends—paintings (from left to right) by Laurens, Albers, and Le Corbusier—envelope the living room. A Tino and Corbu sand-casting collaboration can be seen through the doorway.

Ruth, with her son, Pietro, and grandson, Adrian, are surrounded by hundreds of artworks and models for architectural projects that remain on exhibition in the studio Tino built on the grounds.

109

Ingeborg ten Haeff & John Githens

Living with contemporary art is a way of keeping up with the currents of change.

Their home is a biography of three people. It reflects the aesthetic journey that one woman has made over the course of a half century with two husbands a generation and a world apart. Ingeborg ten Haeff moved into her apartment in the 1830s row house on Washington Square Park in 1953 with her late husband, architect Paul Lester Weiner. They lived in and traveled throughout South America, where she made her first discoveries of the art she and her current husband, translator John Githens, live with in mutual appreciation.

Ingeborg remembers prowling through art and flea markets to find eighteenth-century Cuzco school paintings from colonial Peru and pre-Columbian pottery. "My interest in sacred art and those now treasured *huacos* [pots] was immediate. It was always natural for me to search out beautiful things, and I continued to do so when I traveled with John in Asia and Central America."

Ingeborg built close friendships with many of the architects and artists Weiner brought home—Marcel Duchamp, Herbert Bayer, Richard Lindner, and Le Corbusier. The presence of these extraordinary people in her life is celebrated by the artworks that ornament their apartment today. Ingeborg reminisces, "I remember Miró dancing in our Long Island summer house. We would go to Calder's farm in Connecticut and watch Sandy turn the most ordinary things into kitchen utensils and jewelry that I wear." She calls attention to two mobiles that hover about the bed.

"Meeting Ingeborg was a learning experience for me," John says. "Ingeborg exposed me to the Bauhaus and the New York School, transporting me into a very different world. I discovered that living with contemporary art is a way of keeping up with the currents of change."

A self-taught artist, Ingeborg contributed to their eclectic decor with her abstract expressionist paintings and the nineteenth-century English reading table she found at an auction. A ceremonial Japanese bed doubles as floor art demonstrating her belief that "a person should be able to do everything in every space—sleep, drink, eat, talk, whatever."

111

OPPOSITE, TOP

Ingeborg freely mixes periods and cultures in a multipurpose room that brings together a nineteenth-century English table set with Sylvia Baker's black pottery tableware, a ceremonial Japanese bed, a Cuzco painting, and a ten Haeff abstract expressionist canvas.

OPPOSITE, BOTTOM

Leather-tooled shelves designed by Ingeborg's late husband exhibit objects including pre-Columbian pots and a Chinese vessel. Above are two Cuzco paintings, the left a rare depiction of thirty stations of the cross.

PRIVATE COLLECTIONS

AT HOME TO THE PUBLIC

I am convinced that the true collector does not acquire objects of art for himself alone. . . . Appreciating the beauty of the object, he is willing and even eager to have others share his pleasure. It is, of course, for this reason that so many collectors loan their finest pieces to museums or establish museums of their own where the items they have painstakingly collected may be viewed by the general public.

In a 1965 essay, J. Paul Getty expressed his belief that art collections should be willed to the public and made accessible in intimate environments that enhance the viewing experience. Art critic Robert Hughes reminds us of the comfort we find in small, well-loved museums where the scale is human and the eye is focused, not distracted by masses of people, where there is a "gift of intimacy and unhurried ease in the presence of serious art."

THE FRICK COLLECTION

In his will, Henry Clay Frick dictated that his house along with all its art and furnishings would become the Frick Collection, "a gallery of art to which the entire public shall forever have access." When he built his house on Fifth Avenue, commissioning New York Public Library architect Thomas Hastings, he was determined to make the setting worthy of his idiosyncratic mix of paintings, sculpture, and decorative objects. One can imagine the art aficionado seated in one of the eight Savonarola chairs placed about the long gallery room contemplating Rembrandt, Veronese, Turner, Vermeer, Corot, and El Greco. Frick's biographer, George Harvey, wrote, "Often, late at night, he would slip noiselessly, almost furtively into the darkness of the gallery, turn on the lights and sit for an hour or more . . . absorbing solace and happiness through the mirrors of his heart."

In his Fragonard Room, Henry Clay Frick dedicated the walls to grand canvases by this French master painter.

THE PHILLIPS COLLECTION

The Phillips Collection remains true to the vision of its founder, who opened the gallery rooms of his Washington, D.C., home to the public while he still lived there. "Instead of the academic grandeur of marble halls and stairways . . . we plan to try the effect of domestic architecture, of rooms small or at least livable, and of such an intimate, attractive atmosphere as we associate with a beautiful home," Duncan Phillips wrote. Phillips, who created the first modern-art museum in 1921, eight years before the Museum of Modern Art in New York, was prescient not only in the modern art he acquired but in his thinking: "Now that taste has been corrupted to the point where few can distinguish scale from size, and 'important' means 'unmanageably big,' one is apt to lose sight of the fact that most of the paintings that changed art history between 1860 and 1950 would fit over a fireplace." In addition to a roomful of Bonnard canvases, Phillips collected French impressionist and postimpressionist paintings, which he integrated works by Arthur Dove, John Marin, Alfred Stieglitz, and later, Morris Louis, Mark Rothko, and Kenneth Noland.

THE ISABELLA STEWART GARDNER MUSEUM

At the end of the nineteenth century, Isabella Stewart Gardner specified in her will that after her death nothing be changed in her Venetian palace, Fenway Court, in Boston. A century later we still see, in the Isabella Stewart Gardner Museum, flaming orange nasturtiums in the courtyard and the brocade-covered walls on which she hung her collection of Italian masterpieces mixed with Chinese bronzes, Gothic crucifixes, and Dutch, English, and French paintings. In *The Proud Possessors*, Aline Saarinen says that "the creation of a beautiful environment was to Gardner, an act of virtue. . . . She believed in salvation through taste."

THE BARNES FOUNDATION

A new force in the art world, Dr. Albert Barnes was a self-made man with substantial financial and intellectual resources. He established the Barnes Foundation in 1922 in Marion, Pennsylvania, to "promote the advancement of education and appreciation of fine arts." To design a gallery, he selected French architect Paul Cret, who explained that "the first care has been to secure those conditions that the painter could wish for the display of his work . . . small rooms and studio lighting." The foundation houses an extraordinary number of masterpieces by Renoir (180), Cezanne (69), and Matisse (60). Together with art from every corner of the globe, antique furniture, ceramics, hand-wrought iron, and Native American jewelry, Barnes designed nontraditional art displays to demonstrate the continuity of great art throughout history. In 1938 he wrote, "The way we hang pictures is not the ordinary way: each picture on a wall has not only to fit in a definite unity but it has to be adapted to our purpose of teaching traditions."

THE PEGGY GUGGENHEIM COLLECTION

You don't have to imagine it; you can arrive by gondola at the eighteenth-century Palazzo Venier dei Leoni on the Grand Canal in Venice to view the Peggy Guggenheim Collection. She lived there for thirty years, later opening it to the public as a museum and donating the palazzo and her art collection to the Solomon R. Guggenheim Foundation of New York. Though stripped of furnishings with the exception of a dining room set in the Cubist gallery and the Calder headboard in her bedroom, the palazzo still resonates with the power of Peggy Guggenheim's personality. In it hang art by Cubists, surrealists, European abstractionists, and early American abstract expressionists. Among them are paintings by her protégé, Jackson Pollock, and her husband, Max Ernst.

OLANA

Frederick Church planned and created his Moorish-style mansion, Olana, overlooking the Hudson River in upstate New York with the same artistry that made him America's leading landscape artist in the nineteenth century. James Anthony Ryan, manager of Olana, observed, "one of Church's first aims was to create a repository for the objects of civilization." Poet John Ashbery, who lives a few miles away, described the picture gallery–dining room as "vaguely medieval with its gray-green and maroon plastered walls, brass and teak fireplace, and mixed bag of heavily framed old master paintings," which Church acquired in Europe. Positioned throughout the house are several of Church's own paintings, along with treasures from his travels—a Mexican Madonna, Chinese and Japanese pictures, Persian armor, and Oriental carpets.

WADDESDON MANOR

Many stately English homes and French châteaux, which are open to the public, contain fine ancestral art collections. A striking recently restored example is Waddesdon Manor in Buckinghamshire, England. It was built in the 1870s by Baron Ferdinand de Rothschild to house his collection of porcelain, furniture, and paintings, including eighteenth-century English portraits by Gainsborough and Reynolds and seventeenth-century Dutch master-works. The Rothschild family tended these possessions over many years before handing them over to the National Trust.

SIR JOHN SOANE'S MUSEUM

One of the lesser known jewels in London is Sir John Soane's Museum founded by the celebrated early

The medieval style dining room at Olana doubled as a picture gallery for the display of Frederick Church's collection of old master paintings.

Classical busts, cinerary urns, and architecture fragments are assembled like a scene of Roman ruins under the dome in Sir John Soane's Museum.

In the Wallace Collection, furniture, Sèvres porcelain, and paintings from the Louis XV period represent the rococo style at its most opulent.

nineteenth-century architect of the Bank of England. Since Soane stipulated that his collection should not be disturbed, this museum has retained the authentic character and furnishings of a private house of the period (1813). Most notable of the works on display are the paintings of William Hogarth and the alabaster sarcophagus of Seti I, king of Egypt (circa 1370 B.C.). Antiquities, sculpture, furniture, and architectural drawings as well as canvases by Watteau, Turner, and Canaletto crowd this former home, which is enhanced by the clever use of mirrors.

THE WALLACE COLLECTION

The Wallace Collection, once a private London home, was bequeathed to the British government in 1897 with the stipulation that its contents be displayed to the public and that nothing be added or taken away. Former residents, the Marquesses of Hertford and, later, Sir Richard and Lady Wallace, contributed to this British treasure house, which contains paintings from the Renaissance to the late nineteenth century as well as French furniture, Sèvres porcelain, and European arms and armor.

from

SELF-PORTRAIT
IN A CONVEX MIRROR

JOHN ASHBERY

As Parmigianino did it, the right hand

Bigger than the head, thrust at the viewer

And swerving easily away, as though to protect

What it advertises. A few leaded panes, old beams,

Fur, pleated muslin, a coral ring run together

In a movement supporting the face, which swims

Toward and away like the hand

Except that it is in repose. It is what is

Sequestered. Vasari says, "Francesco one day set himself

To take his own portrait, looking at himself for that purpose

In a convex mirror, such as is used by barbers . . .

He accordingly caused a ball of wood to be made

By a turner, and having divided it in half and

Brought it to the size of the mirror, he set himself

With great art to copy all that he saw in the glass,"

Chiefly his reflection, of which the portrait

Is the reflection once removed.

The glass chose to reflect only what he saw

Which was enough for his purpose: his image

Glazed, embalmed, projected at a 180-degree angle.

Partners in Art

AGNES GUND & DANIEL SHAPIRO

I NOW HAVE A MUCH BETTER
UNDERSTANDING OF WHY HE LIKES
3,000-YEAR-OLD BRONZES.

—AGNES GUND

I HAVE LEARNED A GREAT
DEAL ABOUT CONTEMPORARY
ART FROM AGGIE.

—DANIEL SHAPIRO

When Agnes Gund is introduced as the president of New York's Museum of Modern Art, the inevitable question arises: what kind of art does she have at home? "Living with art and being surrounded by it at the museum, as I am, are very different experiences," she confides. "For my own home I don't have to follow a master plan or be concerned about past history or the future. I just buy what I like."

A "lifelong appreciator of art," Gund owns more than eight hundred artworks, only a portion of which can be seen in her floor-through Park Avenue apartment at one time. Agnes admits to missing certain pieces when they are on loan, like the Jasper Johns map that went to the MOMA for his retrospective show in 1997. "I love having it back," she says, "because three other Johns pieces will be gone for about a year, traveling to other museums." To deal with the comings and goings of art in their home, Agnes once created a "changing wall" in the entranceway. "At one time we placed a large Chia

painting there that friends largely ignored. It went out to a show, but when it came back, they absolutely flipped. They were just so happy to see this painting back in its place again.

"I found that people don't always like change," Agnes says. "But I do. I like to move my pictures around because

OPPOSITE

A hallway composition is enlivened by Rietveld's iconic chair, Jackie Winsor's inset wall piece with stepped black interior, Betty Woodman's whimsical ceramic holding seasonal arrangements, and a proud standing figure from Bambara, Mali, c. 12th–16th centuries.

ABOVE

Agnes and Daniel are cornered by two favorite artists—Tony Smith (left) and Gerhard Richter (right).

Dorothea Rockburne's Robe Series, Sepulchre *over the bedroom mantel covered with family photos and personal art objects.*

it allows me to see them in a different way. It's a privilege to see artworks in various lights, weather, relationships, not to mention one's own moods. There are certain paintings that I have moved from one room to another or stored away for a while, but that doesn't mean that I would want them out of my life forever."

The biggest change, however, came ten years ago when Agnes married Daniel Shapiro, an art lawyer and trustee for the Museum for African Art in New York. Their partnership in marriage resulted in a dynamic art alliance. Daniel slowly integrated his growing collection of Chinese and African antiquities into Agnes's environment of modern art. "I have always been interested in art," Daniel explains, "and spent a great deal of time as a young lawyer at the Freer Gallery in Washington, D.C., where I was transfixed by its Shang bronzes. But it never occurred to me to pursue my own personal course until Aggie introduced me to the satisfaction of living in a house filled with exciting art. A birthday gift she wanted to give me resulted in my first acquisition of African art, a terra-cotta head that captured me, as art objects often do."

Although Aggie and Daniel keep to their separate areas of interest, they admit to having greatly benefited from the different art worlds that each brings to the other. Daniel says, "I have learned a great deal about contemporary art from Aggie." To which Agnes responds, "I now have a much better understanding of why he likes 3,000-year-old bronzes, and I admire the craftsmanship and beauty of the terra-cottas he has collected." Agnes points out that Daniel is interested in art in a different way than she is. "He visits Africa and cultivates friendships there, bringing back new people and viewpoints. When I look at contemporary art in a museum, I take it all in rapidly because I want to see a lot of different things. Daniel, on the other hand, can stand in front of one case of bronzes for a half hour."

Agnes was exposed to art much earlier than Daniel. "I grew up with things on the walls," she remembers. "My father had a very eclectic collection, mainly western art, so I was in tune with visual stuff as a child. We had a great museum in Cleveland, and I took classes there. But the real awakening began with a dedicated art history teacher who would send me posters from places like the Gardner, the Phillips, and the Frick, encouraging me to visit them.

"About a year after my first marriage in the early sixties, I bought a few works by Australian artists when we traveled there. But my art venture really began with the Henry Moore sculpture that I bought in 1967. I remember having nightmares about how much it cost and finally deciding that if I was going to acquire art in a serious way, I should do it with the idea of benefiting museums someday." Agnes achieved her objective when she gave Moore's *Three Way Piece Archer* to the Cleveland Museum of Art, marking the beginning of decades of donations to several leading museums.

At first she thought about collecting old master drawings, which she was drawn to, but decided against it because she would have to live in the dark. "They are light-sensitive and so am I. I need light. I can't have shades drawn, so I decided to concentrate on contemporary art. I wanted to live with art of my time. There were several obvious advantages: I could get to know the artists, and I wouldn't have problems with forgeries."

120

The library in the Gund/Shapiro home is devoted to Daniel's growing collection of Chinese and African antiquities. Pieces from Mali, Tanzania, and the Ivory Coast live in harmony with several of Agnes's modern art treasures—a Gorky painting over the sofa and a Dubuffet over the fireplace.

Agnes says she enjoys the art in her living room every day because it's where she exercises—Rauschenberg's first combine picture above the fireplace, Stella's star-shaped canvas opposite, a Rosenquist through one doorway, a Tipo through the other, a Hoffman inbetween. A Tony Smith sculpture anchors the Giacometti coffee table on a kilim rug.

An assembly of African figures greets you at the front door. A Di Suvero iron sculpture sits on a white cube. Brian Hunt's airship hangs above a Kelly painting. A light piece by Antonakos glows above an explosive Chihuly glass work. Opposite is a wrapped wedding gift by Christo. A floor-to-ceiling Lichtenstein punctuates a corridor lined with art.

Gund recalls going to Mark Rothko's house just before his pieces came to the Marlborough in New York. "I was one of the last people to buy a painting directly from him. I had it when I was pregnant with my third child and lived in Shaker Heights, Ohio. I fell asleep in the living room one day sitting in front of it and thought

ABOVE

Two photographs of Northern Italian aristocrats by Patrick Figenbaum and several children's drawings lead you into a spacious kitchen festooned with a collage of postcards from all over the world.

ABOVE, RIGHT

A corner of the library illustrates the seamless marriage of Daniel and Agnes's collections. A 1949 Jackson Pollock hangs above a Roman desk setting off Chinese vases and an Gigoa cloth-bound African figure.

the change of light was so wonderful that I wrote him about it. He responded, inviting me to visit him, which I did.

"A few years later, when visiting New York, I joined the International Council at the Museum of Modern Art and became very good friends with Emily Tremaine, who took me to a lot of art places and events." Gund cites as critical her decision to forgo buying the formidable Ben Heller collection, which was up for sale. "I have never regretted it, because if I had, I would not have been able to choose the art I discovered myself and live with today.

"Over the years I have collected some things that are great, some that are second-rate, and some that are just tchotchkes that I like to have around, like Tony Berlant's amusing caviar tins." Gund describes herself as a collector who keeps her art, decrying the "sickening" 1980s when everyone started to buy and sell the work of artists like

Johns and de Kooning. "That's when some of the artists got to like me so well, because I was one of the few who didn't sell out. I racked my brain to understand why Jasper Johns would come over to realign the stretchers on his piece for me. I finally figured out why he would do such a wonderful thing. He realized that I enjoyed living with his work and would never sell it. If my Johns piece was worth $17 million at that time, what was I going to buy with all that money—something just as expensive but not as good! Also, if you sell it, you don't have it."

Daniel feels equally passionate about the archaic objects he has brought home. He equates collecting art with an ivory hunter's amulet worn around the neck to help the hunter find game and to protect him. "People think of this act as very primitive," he says, "but it's not that different from what we do today. Human beings have always created rituals and environments to help them deal with their needs and surroundings."

The walls on the upstairs landing of this New York apartment illustrate

the lives of the owners—photographs, drawings, silhouettes, sketches.

The Sargent-like portrait of Monina was painted by Kim Beaty.

MONINA VON OPEL & EDWARD MILLER

EACH PICTURE HAS ITS OWN STORY FOR US, SOMETIMES EVEN IF IT'S JUST THE FRAME.

In some houses the relationship between what furnishes the rooms and what hangs on the walls is so seamless that it is difficult to tell where one leaves off and the other begins. Such is the New York duplex apartment of Edward Miller and Monina von Opel. Art, in this case, is almost another word for personal baggage, the stuff you accumulate, along with your chairs and pillows, to create a feeling of home.

Monina von Opel grew up in Switzerland and France, in houses that never gave her a sense of belonging. She only discovered that sense after she began to live on her own in Paris. "I was introduced to the flea markets of Paris," she says, "and I was hooked. I became the queen of junk." Paul Bert, Boiron, Marché des Puces— these became the places where she found her true loves, bringing furniture, fabrics, paintings, objets d'art, back to her apartment. "I wanted to feather my nest," is how she describes her passion. "Wherever I went, to any city in the world, I traveled with an expandable bag so I could bring things back."

Her taste was eclectic, full of wit and curiosity. "I know what I like instantly," she says. "It's like seeing a man you fancy at a party. You just know! Of course a picture is less risky to pursue than a man. But a picture might cost more. I was always looking for a bargain, either in objects or in paintings."

Edward Miller's early experience of art was very different from Monina's, and so was his taste. "I did not grow up in an artistic environment. I had an epiphany when I was twenty-one years old. I was invited to Sunday lunch by the president of the Philadelphia Museum of Art. It was spring, and the dogwoods were in bloom, and in the garden behind the house was a life-size Picasso sculpture of a man holding a sheep in his arms." The garden was in fact filled with sculpture—Henry Moore, Maillol, Marini, Lachaise, Matisse. On the dining room walls Miller recognized Modigliani, Courbet, Chagall. "It was my first experience of people *living* with art."

Galvanized by the experience, Miller went to a Philadelphia gallery and bought a piece of sculpture, *Dying Bull,* by Aldo Casanova. It was the beginning of his journey into art. For many years he bought sculpture when he could, paying off each piece over time, and learned what he liked best. "It was the touch and feel of it I loved," he said. Gradually, as his career as an investment banker flourished, he expanded his interest to include paintings, such as those by Dubuffet, Kline, Quaytman, Berthot, Avery, and Scully. After an inspiring dinner with Philip Guston, he was immediately driven to collect that artist's work.

Thus when Edward and Monina met twenty years ago, it was the meeting of two very different aesthetics. Monina's easygoing accumulating changed. "I had always walked past abstract art. To me, representational art was

BELOW

The paintings here—a wheel by Philip Guston and a nineteenth-century woman with a parrot that Monina fell in love with—work wonderfully with the multicolored textures and patterns of the room.

BOTTOM

Edward Miller assumed the task of hanging twenty-one Miró prints on the wall of this long corridor. The challenge was compounded by the fact that they were all slightly different in size.

more amusing. But when I met Edward, it became fun to mix. I don't like all modern or all Louis XVI. That's boring. We live in our own time, not in the past." For Edward, Monina's quirky enthusiasms diverted and enhanced his own. Now when they go to a gallery together and ask afterward, "Guess what I liked?" they will come up with the same answers.

Their apartment is vivid confirmation of this happy marriage of interests. It is filled with modern sculpture and paintings along with primitive portraits and textiles from many countries, plus mementos, family photographs, the proof of busy, fulfilled lives. Edward and Monina share decorating decisions about the apartment, although here too their creative styles are very different. "I hang everything by eye," Monina says. "Edward *measures.*" They also move things a lot. "Paintings hide holes in the wall." Moreover, Monina adds, "I think pictures and sculpture *should* get moved. Otherwise you stop seeing them properly."

Just as book lovers constantly complain about running out of shelf space, so these two art lovers are beginning to look in despair at their walls. "We've accumulated so much," Monina sighs. "When I go to the dentist, I used to pass the time by counting the paintings in each of our rooms. I can't do that anymore." Yet it's hard to divest. "Each picture has its own story for us, sometimes even if it's just the frame."

So they still visit galleries and talk about art. Their basic rule is, Can we afford it? Can we live without it? "To me, it's an instant feeling," Edward says, echoing Monina's instinctive response to a work. "Do I wake up in the morning with that *image*? Then I must have it."

Monina sums up their continuing interest in her own way, preferring to focus on paintings, which take up less room than three-dimensional objects and are easier to transport. Like a snail, she likes to feel she can take her house with her on her back. "Paintings are low-maintenance," she says. "That's why I love them."

ABOVE

In this much lived-in room, a portrait of Andrew Jackson at the Battle
of New Orleans by an unknown naive painter hangs over the fireplace.
The bookstack is by Leonid Lerman; the red-over-gray painting is
by Jake Berthot.

OVERLEAF

The kitchen is a delicious marriage of art and eating, watched over by
a Peruvian church painting of St. Ursula. Monina says, "It's an honor
for a painting to be in my kitchen, where I spend so much time."
A small Calder sits on the table.

RAMÓN & NERCYS CERNUDA

OUR INTEREST IN CUBAN ART STEMS FROM OUR ROOTS, A COUNTRY WE HAD TO LEAVE.

Whether you are old enough to be nostalgic about a Cuba you once traveled to or lived in, or young enough to wonder about an island that has been closed to you, a visit to the Cernuda family home in Miami is a singular experience. Upon entering a blazing white condominium, you are confronted by color-intense paintings as Ramón Cernuda invites you to view a unique collection of twentieth-century Cuban art.

Like many other Miami residents, Ramón and Nercys left Cuba with their families as political exiles in the early sixties. "Our interest in Cuban art stems from our roots, the place where we were born, a country we had to leave in our formative years. We have tried to maintain a relationship to our heritage."

"The Cernudas rescued art that could have been lost forever," Carlos Luis, director of Miami's Cuban Museum of Art and Culture wrote in the catalog accompanying the 1988 exhibition of their collection. It has since grown to include 350 works, the majority of which document a rich period in Cuban painting from the 1920s through

the 1960s. Art historians refer to it as the School of Havana since many of the artists lived and worked there. Ramón explains, "We have sought out the work of three generations of these artists who were concerned with expressing national identity, starting with Victor Manuel, who helped launch the modern art movement in Cuba."

In the living room, couches, armchairs, and amusing Cuban Art Deco rockers are arranged to provide a sweeping view of four startling paintings. This room is a gathering place for family, friends, and the international art community in which the Cernudas are involved. Ramón, who has been active with the Cuban Museum for fifteen years, explains, "We're not only collectors but promoters of Cuban art, helping to fund exhibitions and supporting art history research."

Within view of the living room is the Cernuda library. French doors open to reveal Ramón's study, which contains books, catalogs, and magazines devoted to the history of Cuban art, along with the educational materials the Cernudas publish to teach English to the Spanish-speaking community.

OPPOSITE

Every room, including walkways throughout the house, is hung with twentieth-century Cuban art. At the end of a crowded corridor is The Fools, *a portrait by Arturo Rodriguez of his wife and himself. On the left is a portrait of Cuban journalist Adela Jaume, by Jorge Arche.*

Reflected in the piano is a famous Enríquez surrealist painting of a nineteenth-century Robin Hood character, the legendary Cuban bandit Manuel Garcia.

Ramón and Nercys have found most of their artworks at galleries and auction houses, frequently in the United States though occasionally in Europe or Latin America. They purchased their first major piece, a Fidelio Ponce oil, at Christie's in 1982. They placed it in an unexpected alcove at the end of a hallway, one of several art retreats they have designed to encourage intimate contemplation of particular paintings.

"That first auction was a real eye opener," Nercys remembers. "Seeing so much beautiful art, not only Cuban but Latin American art all together was like attending a seminar. Back then we were a small group, mostly Latin Americans. It was like a private club. Every six months we went to New York and several of us became friends through the art we were looking for."

"However, the auction scene has now changed," Ramón adds. "It has lost its intimacy. It's more competitive and global. We are seeing not only more people, Europeans and Asians, but younger people, like our children."

Ramón and Nercys are proud that their twenty-two-year-old daughter, Gined, and their seventeen-year-old son, Sergio, have input in the decisions regarding the art they buy. "Finding art is a family project," Ramón says. "Our children are adamant about the art they want in their rooms, have strong opinions about where certain paintings look best, and frequently accompany us to auctions."

Sergio breaks in, "Last year when my parents went to New York, I told them to go for the most expensive painting instead of several smaller ones for the same amount of money. And that's just what they did."

Ramón responds with amusement, "We bought the large Portocarrero painting that now hangs in the entry hall. It was the most expensive Cuban painting we were considering. I remember Sergio saying, 'Let's go for the touchdown.' And although we hesitated because it was a big investment, we decided he had the right strategy."

Gined, who now lives in Seattle, recalls: "Beyond the historical and political relevance of the art we grew up with, it was the imagery that really affected me, like *The Broken Child* by Demi that I chose for my bedroom and *Eva,* the painting by Carlos Enríquez that hangs in the living room. I'm a dancer, so I like the motion and energy of Enríquez's work." She adds, "It wasn't until all the art was removed in that dreadful FBI raid that I realized what a presence it was in my life."

Ramón explains, "It was a nightmare for our family. In August of 1989 fourteen agents broke down our doors as if they were conducting a drug raid and took all the art off our walls. They claimed that we were in violation of the embargo laws that impede Cuban products from coming into the United States. I explained that we had not acquired any works from the Cuban government or Cuban nationals because Nercys and I have not been allowed to go back there since we left. I had provenance files on every painting that proved where they came from, which the FBI confiscated as well. We sued the government in federal court and got a quick ruling stating that art is constitutionally protected as a means of conveying information. It meant so much to all of us to not only get the artwork back but to have Judge Kenneth Ryskamp say that, like free speech, art is protected by the First Amendment."

In the living room, the Cernuda family below paintings by (from left to right) *Angel Acosta León, Mariano Rodríguez, Fidelio Ponce, and Carlos Enríquez.*

ROBERT & LYNN JOHNSTON

I LOVE TO STAND IN THE LIVING ROOM
AND *FEEL* THE COLOR.

What makes people respond to one kind of art rather than another? To Kenneth Noland's targets rather than Monet's water lilies? Perhaps fortunately, there is no simple answer. But in the case of Lynn and Robert Johnston, a combination of form and color is clearly their preferred visual taste, a mixture distilled from their two personalities, as delightful as fine wine.

Bob Johnston's background was in engineering. Courses at Princeton University triggered his interest in art, and his first purchases were, perhaps not surprisingly for an engineer, the geometric works of artists such as Vasarely and Albers. He also had a tendency toward the macabre and was drawn to the work of Rico Lebrun. After becoming an investment banker in New York City, Bob visited galleries and expanded his taste. Moving on from the abstract forms of his early graphics, he came to be interested in more representational work, buying a lithograph by Rouault, for instance, which the Johnstons still own.

Meanwhile, Lynn, the child of well-traveled parents who brought back paintings and objects from Asia, was more traditional in her taste, loving the French impressionists. When she and Bob got together, an interesting aesthetic fusion took place. He abandoned his pure geometry and became drawn to big canvases, strong in form and shape, buying pictures on gut instinct. She developed her powerful response to color, finding herself attracted to the works of John Walker, Joan Snyder, and Dorothea Rockburne, for instance. "We came to art as others go to the opera," Lynn says of their early enthusiastic forays into the art world.

After living in New York, the couple, with a growing family, moved to Princeton, where "we had a whole house to fill up," Lynn says. But they were extremely fastidious in their purchases, buying only what they really wanted, so "for a year there wasn't much on the walls." The first house they bought was in the French Provincial style; the color scheme was soft and neutral except for a Chinese red dining room. In 1994 the Johnstons bought a seventeenth-century New Jersey farmhouse on thirty-two

137

The relationship between the colors in the Joan Snyder painting and the colors of the furnishings create a brilliant effect.

138

acres with two ponds and a romantic creek. The challenge they then confronted was how to make the space work for their family and their love of art.

With the New York architectural firm of Stamberg and Aferiat, they gutted the farmhouse, so that the open space not only worked as a family house but also embraced their paintings and the beautiful landscape. Yet although there was a definite transition within the interior from traditional to contemporary, it was accomplished without entirely abandoning the sense of scale that was part of the legacy of the old farmhouse.

All the participants had strong feelings about the use of color in the new space. There was never any doubt in the Johnstons' minds that the paintings would enhance— and be enhanced by—the colors on the walls. They liked the architects' suggestion of a basic "spine" of yellow, and the other colors seemed to follow naturally—terra-cotta in the dining area, purple and orange in the living room, and red in the hall. It is a remarkable exercise in harmony.

Impulse and good luck also play a part. In the living

room the dramatic purple on the wall opposite the fireplace was copied from a purple ribbon Lynn loved. It was not until later that she purchased the Joan Snyder painting, although it works so well against the striking purple backdrop that one might suppose they had been designed to go together. "I love to stand in the living room and *feel* the color," Lynn says.

In an intelligent move, the Johnstons took photographs of all the art in their old house, so they could plan roughly where every picture would hang in the new one. "We knew, for instance, that we would hang the Rouault over the fireplace in the dining area. For a start, that gave us a focus and sense of color for the rest of the space." The wide-open kitchen, formerly five little rooms, was another important place earmarked for pictures. "I wanted to live with art in my kitchen, since we spend so much time there," Lynn points out.

If it is Lynn who contributes the eye for brilliant color that permeates the jewel-like house, it is Bob who injects the sense of surprise and adventure. The Johnstons travel a lot with their three children and have collected all sorts of artworks as a result of their adventures: saddlebags from Santa Fe, a Burmese Buddha, Khmer pieces, a Chinese robe, American Indian masks from the Northwest. "I once suggested to Lynn that we make a serious collection of one subject, such as the Constructivists of the late twenties and thirties," Bob recalls. "But it was hopeless. We are truly eclectic."

Lynn agrees. "Bob likes chocolate, vanilla, *and* strawberry ice cream."

"We are branching out now into sculpture," Bob says, pointing out the Kenneth Snelson, Arnaldo Pomodoro, and George Rickey works outside in the parklike garden. Looking at the intricate designs of these sculptures, one gets the feeling that Bob, while moving far from the geometric prints he started out with, is yet in a way still fascinated by masterpieces of artistic engineering. Thus even in this uncompromisingly eclectic household, there is a sense of continuity.

BELOW

The main hallway of the house, with its original staircase, is an elegant combination of color and shape, echoing the art. The two glass vases are by Sonja Blomdahl.

OVERLEAF

The orange wall in the foreground, the reds in the John Walker painting, and the purples and yellows in the Joan Snyder canvas over the sofa create a ribbon of color in the living room. Two Louise Nevelsons on the far wall accentuate the visual drama of the space.

SONDRA GILMAN & CELSO GONZALEZ-FALLA

IT HAD EVERYTHING TO DO WITH LOOKING, LOOKING, LOOKING, BECAUSE THE EYE EDUCATES ITSELF.

Few things reveal as much about Sondra Gilman as her story about the painting that covers the entire living room wall in her town house in New York. This 1969 Frank Stella work, *Hagmatana 1,* was her first art purchase, one she had the courage to buy when she was a newly married woman in her twenties. "I was dazzled by it. When I marched into Leo Castelli's, I knew even then it was a masterpiece, and Leo spent about three hours telling me why. He was so convincing, I thought I should buy two. I ended up doing just that!"

Sondra had some persuading to do before she sent the paintings home. "My late husband, Charles Gilman Jr., understood the modern masters and had strong feelings about Degas and van Gogh, so it was natural that he would hesitate. He told me he could live with the second painting I wanted, one of a series from Stella's *Polish Synagogue,* but not the one I had fallen in love with. I urged him to 'live with it for six months. If you don't like it after that, we'll sell it.' At the end of two months, it was his favorite."

The same understanding and respect dictate the purchase of art for Gilman and Gonzalez-Falla's homes today. After Sondra's first husband died and she remarried, the acquisition of art continued to require mutual agreement. "If either Celso or I veto something, it's vetoed. We try to talk about it, but if we don't succeed, we don't buy it. We've found there is enough art we both enjoy, and fortunately we have room for it in our three very different homes."

Sondra and Celso are in the land development business and have discovered that art sensibilities change when you live in different parts of the country, as they do. The art they are choosing for their newest home, in southern Georgia, reflects their determination to sustain the tranquil environment of the lakeside house. Photographs of sky and water by Richard Misrach, Hiroshi Sugimoto, and Jack Pierson contribute to the "total Zen look" that Celso and Sondra are creating here.

Sondra explains that their home in New York, where she has spent most of her life, has many works by artists who live there or are represented by New York galleries.

OPPOSITE

A stairwell that climbs five flights serves as a gallery for a step-by-step chronology of an international assembly of master photographers.

ABOVE

A view of the opposite wall. In the foreground, a table set with quixotic objets d'art—Richard Shaw's Book Jar with Shaw's Finger Paints *and Betty Woodman's* Sikkin (Still Life Vase).

LEFT

Sondra's first major art purchase, Stella's Hagmatana 1, *is reflected in the mirror above the Victorian marble fireplace in their parlor where two color-saturated Warhol silkscreens, an icon floral image and a portrait of Sondra, ricochet off red walls.*

Incongruous as it may seem, huge canvases by Andy Warhol, Ellsworth Kelly, Kenneth Noland, Peter Halley, and Neil Jenney coexist in ballroom-size twin living rooms decorated with French furniture and bridged by a haunting Edward Ruscha painting and a whimsical Frank Gehry fish lamp. "It's a challenging art environment that is appropriate to New York," Sondra says.

In sharp contrast, they describe their home in Texas as "sort of funky." Celso was born in Cuba, lived in Texas, and went to college there, so their home in Corpus Christi is filled with Tex-Mex furniture and embraces western art. "I'm not talking about Remington," Sondra says, "but contemporary artists, mostly young ones, who

A 1985 painting by one of their favorite artists, Andy Warhol, is displayed against a backdrop of rare Chinese paper in the dining room. "Where else would you put a picture of Campbell's Soup," Sondra says.

146

live on the West Coast, in the Southwest, or in Texas." They have established a foundation to encourage these regional artists.

"Our attitude toward art is that nobody owns anything," Sondra says. "We are simply caretakers. Many of our paintings are requested for museum shows, and of course it's important to lend them. But I miss them, and it destroys me to have to move things around so often, especially since we do the hanging ourselves. This became the impetus for us to focus on our other passion, photography—photographs are so much easier to change around."

You wouldn't think so when you see the way Sondra and Celso have arranged hundreds of them in the stairwell gallery of their New York town house. Collected over three decades, the photographs are hung edge to edge from the first stair tread to the fifth-floor library. In addition to three Atgets, the first photographs Sondra bought in the 1970s, the works of every major photographer, from Ansel Adams to Edward Weston, from Jacques

Lartique to Sally Mann, and every genre from Robert Frank to Robert Mapplethorpe are represented.

"Photography is an art form that you can be intimate with," Celso says. "You can have a more personal relationship with a photograph than you can with a painting. You can hold a legendary Steichen, Stieglitz, Strand, or Henri Cartier-Bresson in your hand and view it up close, as you can do when you climb the stairs at a voyeur's pace. A stairway wall is the perfect setting for a photography collection," he adds. "It provides a continuous wall space, and the photographs are protected from direct light."

One hundred works from the couple's photography collection are scheduled to go on tour for two years to museums in college towns throughout the country. "Our goal," Sondra explains, "is to have what happened to me happen to young people. There is no attitude in photography yet, so it's a good place to start a collection. You don't have to be rich for the photography gallery people to be responsive to you. I can still remember the first time I walked into a gallery. My eye wasn't used to it and nothing made sense, but I kept coming back. Eventually I would say, 'I like this artist better than that one,' and it had everything to do with looking, looking, looking, because the eye educates itself."

Sondra recalls giving a lecture on fine art at the High Museum in Atlanta and being asked, "How do you know when you want to buy something?" She answered, "When I stand in front of something and my stomach flips over, then I know it's for me. When I fall in love with a painting, I have to have it. It is never a question of whether it will hold its value; I've never sold a painting or photograph that I've bought. Celso thinks I'm attracted to the works that are hardest to understand. He may be right. The ones you get immediately, you don't look at anymore. They've already told you their secrets."

TOP

Sondra and Celso sit on a settee beneath a haunting photo-realist painting, Edward Ruscha's Affiliation. *Perched on a pedestal, a Frank Gehry fish lamp.*

ABOVE

Two aggressive artworks—Frank Stella's Botofogo 1 (1975), *his first piece using metal, and Mike and Doug Starn's* Yellow Horse and Rider of Artemesion—*share a 20-foot wall in a salon filled with Louis XIV and XV furniture. Peter Halley's Day-Glo painting,* Sylvester, *lights up the adjoining wall.*

The living room reflects a combination of European and Californian influences. The painting over the fireplace is by local artist Dan McCleary, after Vermeer, while the furniture and fabrics are a mixture of European antique and local styles.

SAM WATTERS & DAVID EIDENBERG

WHY WOULD YOU ALWAYS FEEL THE SAME WAY ABOUT PICTURES?

What happens when an art lover changes horses midstream, so to speak, and becomes attracted to different kinds of art from those he has collected assiduously over half a lifetime? Perhaps the break has not quite the drama and complexity of changing partners, but in Sam Watters's case, it was both geographical and emotional, and the house in Santa Monica, California, which he shares with psychologist David Eidenberg, is a fascinating reflection of the path taken—and not taken—to this new destination.

Sam Watters used to live in New York, where he had a large apartment filled with museum-quality pictures and objects. He started young, the child of a family steeped in fine art appreciation. The first picture he ever bought for himself was a drawing of the Paris opera house ceiling by Isodor Pils, which cost him $200 and which he still owns. Gradually he began to make more adventurous purchases, acquiring ancient bronzes, Biedermeier and 1930s furniture, silver, porcelain, old masters, and neoclassical paintings. A scholar in all these fields, he read, studied, visited museums, and carefully assembled his collection. "The controlling force of any collection is taste, and my taste has always been quite specific," Sam explains. "It isn't about building a museum or acquiring social status. It's about finding what you truly like."

But having acquired so much so brilliantly, Sam discovered there was a hollow core to his achievement. "The biggest disappointment for me," he recalls, "was ownership. I loved the hunt and learning about the various pieces I was interested in. That was a pleasure. But ownership is about maintenance and care. That slows you down. People build their lives around this activity. I discovered that, for me, that was a limitation."

Almost every item in Sam's New York apartment has now been sold, and Sam himself has abandoned the city. For two years he and David Eidenberg have slowly been putting together a very interesting and eclectic collection of paintings and objects that they live with in their California house, a comfortable Moorish-style mini-palace on a steep hill overlooking the ocean. Some of the furniture and the art on the walls comes from family and friends. A few pieces are old favorites. The rest they buy from local artists or unknown ones. The result is an expression of the personal taste of two individuals who are very much at ease in their hospitable surroundings.

David Eidenberg brings to the partnership his own sensibility, developed at home with an artist mother. David grew up surrounded by painters and always loved the excitement of the art world in southern California. This aesthetic could hardly be more different from Sam's strongly European-influenced cultural background, but although the two bring very different artistic experiences to the party, the combination is very satisfactory. "We collaborate well," they agree. They tend to prefer representational art to the purely abstract, and, dog lovers par excellence, they buy almost anything with a dog in it.

"Sam is bolder in his color sense than I am," David observes. "On the other hand, I'm much more willing to be whimsical and more informal." David is also less structured when it comes to the use of space. While Sam might object that there is no more room on a wall for a

Sam's library is saturated with color. The painting over the fireplace is a portrait of Saint Mark by one of Leonardo da Vinci's circle, Bernardi Zenale. The two watercolors are nineteenth-century American, the candlesticks by Ohio potter J. Mendez.

ABOVE

The view out of the kitchen window competes cheerfully with a nineteenth-century English painting of two red oxen who won prizes for their Christmas weight in 1868, a photograph of cows by Curtice Taylor, and a nineteenth-century oil of a sheep.

ABOVE, RIGHT

The stairwell displays some of the owners' most personal pictures, including gifts to each other and a painting by Don Eddy, the first serious piece they bought together. The window is like a work of art itself in this intimate gallery.

151

new acquisition or that it does not suit the available space, David will somehow find a place to fit it in harmoniously.

Sam is still experimenting with the difference between acquiring art and living with it. "To me the challenge lies in wanting our house to look comfortable and not precious, and also to be accommodating enough for the dogs. Yet how do you reconcile that with a collection of fine art?" After so many years of being surrounded by the most rarefied art, he is finally discovering a new freedom with regard to what he buys. "It's a pleasure now," he says. "I am less acquisitive and more selective. I no longer care about people knowing who the artist is or was. I used to be very anxious about attribution. Now all I care about is that it is not a fake. All the pieces David and I have bought are very personal. Our taste is always evolving. Why would you always feel

the same way about pictures? There are paintings that we still like but now would never buy."

Perhaps the secret is that, as Sam says, "You have to buy with your heart. There's something that drives us when we see something we like a lot. It's not just an urge to acquire; neither is it a decorative device. We could own something by a famous artist and also a painting nobody has ever heard of—a Matisse drawing, say, and a landscape by a regional artist." In the end, it is the serious art that holds up and resonates for ever. "All other art is decorative and just doesn't sustain the interest."

ANJELICA HUSTON & ROBERT GRAHAM

I FEEL VERY MUCH BACKED BY

MY ANCESTORS.

The life of an actress generally runs counter to the notion of domesticity and a conventional home life. Anjelica Huston has found a way around this instability by carrying her house with her wherever she goes. Brought up in Ireland, with stints in New York, London, and Los Angeles, she simply traveled with her favorite objects as she moved around the world, finally bringing them home to the heart of Venice, California, where she now lives with her husband, sculptor Robert Graham.

They have lived in this house for two years. An oasis of serenity, it was created for Anjelica by Robert. She had lived in the hills and still has a ranch in the foothills of the Sequoia National Park. Her husband wanted to give her something very different but equally dramatic. Not surprisingly, having a sculptor as your architect produces remarkable results. Graham designed the house like a Moorish compound, with a courtyard, trees, tiled staircases, an interior pool, white stucco arches, columns, and domes. "I wanted high walls," Anjelica says. He gave her a secret garden, walls and all.

Inside, the house is flooded with light from windows and balconies, illuminating the myriad pieces of Anjelica's

OPPOSITE

On Anjelica's desk sits a torso by Graham, an Oscar, and a glass collection. Overlooking the display is an early Greek religious icon that belonged to her mother, Ricki.

life—furniture, pictures, and photographs inherited from family and friends, including gifts from her days with Jack Nicholson and mementos from her many movies. Like a jigsaw puzzle, when you put the pieces together a vivid picture emerges of the woman behind that powerful screen image we have come to admire so much.

The two personalities who most clearly define Anjelica within the protected walls of this house are her father, the film director John Huston, and her mother, Ricki, who was married to Huston from 1950 until her tragic death in a car crash in 1969. Photographs of Anjelica's father and mementos of his films, plus art treasures and objects loved by her mother, imbue this house with a sense of rootedness that is in marked contrast to the volatile environment in which she lives. Anjelica's friend Lizzie Spender once visited Anjelica and observed how much Ricki, with her love of an eclectic mix of mother-of-pearl tea chests, perfume bottles, drawings, and photographs, had influenced her daughter's style.

Anjelica has taken some visual themes even farther than her mother, religious art in particular. "I like madonnas and saints and otherworldly esoterica," Anjelica says. "In my ranch in the country I have a wall of weathered angels. Of course, if you have the name Anjelica, you tend to accumulate angels." When she falls in love with something, often at local flea markets and swap meets, she buys it compulsively and seems to find it impossible

RIGHT

In Anjelica's dressing room, a Russian mirrored cabinet holds mementos. At left is a charcoal portrait of Anjelica by Mats Gustafson.

BELOW

Mexican and Greek religious objects surround two favorite pictures— a dog by Charles Van Den Eycken and an ink drawing by Pavel Tchelitchew.

154

to part with. She is drawn to subtle colors in art and textiles and likes to quote Maerose, the character she played in *Prizzi's Honor,* directed by her father: "Everybody sees shapes differently, but colors are forever."

Perhaps the living room is the least Anjelica-like of all the rooms, being the public space and therefore shared between husband and wife. Here Robert Graham's exquisite small bronzes sit alongside wedding gifts, art objects, and works by artist friends such as David Novros. "I overcrowded my rooms with stuff that doesn't mean anything to anybody except me," she explains. "But I subscribe to the Irish policy of the best being saved for the parlor."

The house is hers. There is no doubt about that. " Bob is a minimalist," she says as she walks through the rooms, laughing. "It is quite clear I am the opposite." It is also clear that the sculptor, whose studio is separated from the house by a few hundred yards, has willingly

ceded priority to his wife within these walls.

"I don't collect art," Robert Graham says categorically. "I get given things." Graham designed the Roosevelt memorial in Washington and a salute to Duke Ellington sited in New York City's Central Park. He is at work on other monumental projects, and he also makes small sculptures, mostly torsos, that are hungrily seized upon by his many admirers. His studio is full of sketches and works in progress. "I like the natural accumulation of things and never try to adjust them," he says.

In a recent interview, Anjelica Huston, in observing how many Americans lacked a sense of history, recognized her good fortune in being a Huston, a member of a family blessed with a strong theatrical and film legacy. "I feel very much backed by my ancestors," she said. That legacy continues to animate the house that Robert Graham has so splendidly created for her.

BELOW

In a corner of Robert Graham's studio, his own work, both sculptures and drawings, is vividly revealed in its various stages of development.

BELOW, RIGHT

Wreathed in cigar smoke, Robert Graham coolly surveys his works in progress.

RIGHT

A white corridor leads to the dining room, where a colorful David Novros canvas dominates the far wall, its reds and yellows in a lively dialogue with the colors in the kilim rug on the floor.

BELOW

An extensive collection of photographs and pictures relating mostly to Anjelica's father, John Huston, and her mother, Ricki, cover the walls of the billiard room, forming a visual autobiography of the actress's family life.

OPPOSITE

The Commedia del'Arte tapestry on the far wall of the living room formerly hung in John Huston's bedroom in Ireland. The Chinese scroll on the right is a gift of Harrison and Melissa Ford. Bronzes by Robert Graham stand on the coffee table.

156

JOHN & MARGARET ROBSON

I WAKE UP EVERY DAY AND EXERCISE WHERE I CAN LOOK AT THEM.

The definition of art is constantly subject to reexamination and reevaluation. But few contest the validity and aesthetic value of a kind of art that was almost completely unfamiliar to the public until ten years ago—what is called outsider art, vernacular art, Art Brut, or visionary art.

What is outsider art anyway? John and Margaret Robson explain it very simply. "It is work done by artists with no formal training." Nonetheless, much of the work in the Robsons' San Francisco town house shows technique that is very skilled indeed. The Robsons point out that the artists are in many cases poor rural African-Americans who found a creative outlet through these extraordinary canvases and sculptures, often communicating a kind of spiritual fervor.

The Robsons' entrée into this form of art came in the 1960s, when John Robson was practicing law in Chicago. Unenthusiastic about art ("My mother was a docent at the Art Institute of Chicago," he recalls, "and when growing up, I did everything in my power to avoid having to go to an art museum!"), the first outsider art the Robsons saw and loved was a piece by William Traylor that they found in the 1970s. They started taking a more serious interest in these artists, visiting galleries and

dealers, and they bought steadily. "We are *not* collectors, however," John Robson says firmly. "To be a collector sounds pretentious. We just like the stuff."

In 1993 the Robsons moved to San Francisco. Here, their paintings are mostly hung against plain white walls. "These paintings are part of our life," John says. "I wake up every day and exercise where I can look at them. I think that it is the humor and earthiness in them that I like more than anything." The Robsons' house was once a church, called the Home of Truth. Perhaps that is not an unsuitable name for the strangely moving artworks that are displayed within.

159

OPPOSITE

In the hallway of the Robsons' town house hangs this typical work of outsider artist Ken Grimes, whose themes are always related to outer space and rendered in black and white.

ABOVE

The austere decor of this room pays tribute to the animal pictures by William Traylor, the carved figures by Ulysses Davis, and the stone heads by David Marshall.

The Complete Picture

How to Frame Art

These virtuoso frames in Petworth House, Sussex, are by Grinling Gibbons (1648–1721), the great English baroque wood-carver.

Should every picture be in a frame? Our first impulse is to think so, just as every lamp should have a shade. But with the rise of modern art, traditional frames, like every other aspect of picture-hanging, have been challenged, and new techniques are now offering far more variety.

Prior to the twentieth century, most pictures were framed. The earliest frames were made as part of the painting. The Robert Lehman Collection in New York's Metropolitan Museum contains two very early examples: a pair of paintings by Simone Martini dated 1326, surrounded by simple gold frames with red and blue decoration. By the mid-fifteenth century frames were generally designed independently of the work. Collectors in the seventeenth and eighteenth centuries were accustomed to seeing their treasures displayed in richly gilded and beautifully carved surrounds that were of a piece with the elaborate furniture and fabrics of the period. Some collectors even had a specially designed signature frame that identified them with their pictures.

These kinds of antique frames are still most commonly used for classical art and are often so exquisite that they inspired Robert Lehman to collect almost 350 of them, dating from the fourteenth to the twentieth century. He used some for his pictures and others for his drawings; still others he bought simply as beautiful objects to be admired in their own right. Many of them are periodically exhibited in the Lehman Pavilion of the Metropolitan Museum, offering a fascinating display of different design ideas for art lovers to take home.

The twentieth century has revolutionized the craft of framing. Framers have broken away from the conventions of the past, such as framing impressionist art in baroque gilded frames. Contemporary works on paper, for instance, call out for minimal aluminum or wood frames, or Plexiglas affixed by simple clips. Many contemporary artists claim their canvases look better unframed. Other artists, such as Edward Hicks, who painted many versions of *Peaceable Kingdom*, and Whistler, like to design the frame to go with their work. British artist Howard Hodgkin

The ornate Adam mirror, dating from the 1780s, makes a dramatic contrast to the simple gold frames that Laurence Strenger chose for his nineteenth-century prints and drawings.

paints his pictures already in the frame, with the brush-work spilling out of the canvas and onto the frame as part of the whole visual concept.

Kirk Varnedoe, director of the department of painting and sculpture at New York's Museum of Modern Art, has been systematically reframing the pictures in the post-impressionist galleries, which suffered from a "cacophony" of frames. Some were too elaborate for the paintings, he explained. Others were too austere. "I wanted to reconquer more of the picture as window." To do this, Varnedoe enlisted the help of framing consultant W. H. Bailey and Bark Frameworks, and each individual painting was studied to work out how best to present the work. For instance, three Seurat landscapes now have uniform frames of lay-ered, textured wood, each painted a subtle shade of white that harmonizes with the sky or water in the paintings. Varnedoe says they reflect Seurat's own frame choices.

New York dealers Halley Harrisburg and Michael Rosenfeld believe that you cannot separate the frame from the art. "In the 1970s framing had to be minimal," they explain. "The idea was to let the art speak for itself." These art experts regard this idea as nonsense: "When you buy an important piece of art, it should be framed like an important piece of art. The frame doesn't com-pete; it makes you see the work better."

Cynthia Polsky (see page 101) points out that Indian art, for instance, was not really meant to be framed at all. "Doris Wiener, a dealer of Indian art, started a tradition of framing things in brass frames because they didn't interfere with the art. It's a bit like putting art into a white room, an abstract setting, so you can focus on the work itself." Yet Mrs. Polsky now admits she is using more elab-orate gilded and painted frames. "When I frame anything now, it is definitely more decorative."

In short, framing art is as subjective an issue as buying art. "Don't be afraid of framing," urge Harrisburg and Rosenfeld. "Creative framing can turn a good work into a great one." Jared Bark, founder of Bark Frameworks, stresses the need for balance. "The frame should be well made, pleasing, and discreet. There can exist a visual

African-American artist William Hawkins, who painted this cat, always made his own frames to match his pictures. (From the collection of John and Margaret Robson in San Francisco.)

Photographer Timothy Greenfield-Sanders prefers paintings without frames, although sometimes, as in this large work by Mike and Doug Starn, the frame is inseparable from the art. Other artwork of friends—(from left to right) Ross Bleckner, David Salle, Haim Steinbach, and Richmond Burton—complement his Mission furniture.

interaction between the frame and the work within the frame, but the frame's function is always to be a platform for the work."

Frames transform not only pictures but also entire rooms. A modest white-painted wall can leap to life if hung with a set of botanicals in simple gold frames. A dull corner can be enlivened by a black-and-white photograph framed in a wide black band. A set of similar frames can pull a disparate collection of prints together into a harmonious decorative pattern.

Here are a few guidelines for choosing a frame:

• Get to know the art. Jared Bark believes that "frames are in the service of the artwork." In other words, the frame should not overwhelm the picture or draw the eye away from the picture. "The frame must deal directly with the artwork," he explains. This means understanding the artwork, not only in its own context—that is, where and when it was created—but what it means to you, the owner.

• Study the conventions of framing at the time your artwork was made. An old ancestral portrait would traditionally have been hung in a decoratively carved and gilded frame. Do you want to maintain that reference? For a photograph from the British Raj in India, for instance, you might choose a frame that refers back to that period and subject matter. If it is a contemporary piece, does it requires a frame at all? The important point is that the frame should never be obvious in its reference. Its job is simply to present the work in the best possible way.

• Decide where the artwork is going to hang. Jared Bark does not believe in taking the decorative environment too seriously, however. "You may want to move the picture at some point," he says, "in which case it is a waste of time to try and make it fit into a certain decorative scheme." On the other hand, he points out, if all the moldings in your room are mahogany, it does not make sense to choose a maple frame. "But always avoid the impression you are trying to match something and failing."

• Go to art museums and galleries and study their framing choices. What you see on their walls can be very instructive and can provide ideas. Staff members at galleries can also offer advice.

• If your picture is going to hang on a wall with others, you should take into account the other frames, so that there is not too much dissonance.

• Try to imagine what will best set off your picture. A simple painting may look wonderful in a gilded frame. A complex lithograph may be enhanced by an austere metal frame. An abstract work may not need a frame at all. The goal is for the frame to invite you into the picture. The right frame, in Jared Bark's words, is a question of "restraint and balance."

• Will the frame alter the size of the picture? If the frame encroaches upon the artwork, for instance, is something lost?

• If you have the opportunity, consult the artist whose work you have purchased. Photographer Timothy Greenfield-Sanders admits that "frames tend to distance the work for me. I prefer to have the artist tell me how a work should be framed. Julian Schnabel told me how to hang his painting."

• Visit your local framer. Many retail framers in towns and cities can do a reliable job at a reasonable price. Some professional framers have a repertoire of frames that refer back to historical styles, and can make gilded wood frames based on antique moldings. Other framers offer less expensive ornamentation, color, and size. Many framers are knowledgeable and can guide you. By talking to them and looking at how they have framed the prints on their walls, you can avail yourself of their expertise. When in doubt, seek a simple frame.

• Remember that with works on paper, how you frame your picture has an enormous effect on its longevity. Conservation specialist Martina Yamin says that the number one problem she encounters arises from inexperienced framers. "Without them, we'd be out of business," she says. The use of masking tape, bad glue, nonacidic paper, incorrect matting board, and placing the art too close to the frame are some of the mistakes made in a frame store. She believes that all artworks framed prior to the 1980s, when newer technologies became available, should be opened and examined by a conservator. She adds that sometimes young artists use cheap frames because they can't afford better ones, and these artworks, too, should be looked at.

Paintings

• Always make sure the frame is separated from the painted surface of the picture, because the frame may rub against the paint and damage it. Conservators place cushioning strips between the frame and the picture to avoid this problem.

• Insulated, waterproof, impact-resistant backing is a good protective measure when your picture is framed. This provides insulation against water and air damage and will protect the picture when it is moved.

John Wilde, who painted the still life hanging in the New York City kitchen of Halley Harrisburg and Michael Rosenfeld, also made its frame. A free-floating Ossorio congregation hangs on the right.

• Putting your painting under glass is a subjective call. The effectiveness of an oil painting is diminished when it is seen through glass, but with new glazing technologies such as heat-tempered safety glass with anti-reflective coating and various UV-filtering acrylic materials, which protect against a tropical climate, for instance, such a decision may be more acceptable. Under no circumstances should the glass touch the surface of the painting.

Works on Paper

Because of their delicacy, works on paper require special treatment in matting and framing. Acid-free materials should be used. Make sure your framer knows these requirements.

• Matting—the hard board that acts as a window for the picture—has seen some major changes. Usually a white or off-white window mat is chosen to set off an artwork, but a dark mat can make a pale drawing stand out. Mats come in many colors now, although professionals tend to discourage too much color in a mat (such as picking out the blue that appears as a tiny speck in a painting of a child's dress), as it is likely to overwhelm the painting. New materials have also given framers a vast array of opportunities to mat a work of art creatively. Robert Mapplethorpe sometimes matted his flower photographs with watered silk to enhance the beauty of the images.

Traditionally, a window mat encloses the four edges of the artwork. Today, a popular alternative with collectors,

164

A powerful painting by Philippine artist Manuel Ocampo in an equally powerful wood frame dominates the dining room of Maurice Tuchman, who founded the nineteenth- and twentieth-century art department at the Los Angeles County Museum of Art.

Man Ray's Rayographs, in their black mats, harmonize with a black and white sculpture by Cuban artist, Augustine Cardenas.

under glass or Plexiglas, because of their fragility. Since light causes the most damage to drawings and watercolors, UV-filtering glass or acrylic can help stem deterioration. Conservators say that light damage is cumulative and irreversible.

Photographs

While most of the same rules apply to photographs as to works on paper, photographs do require some special attention: because improper printing and processing can cause them to deteriorate, the temperatures should be kept as constant as possible with low humidity.

Hanging Devices

• Most framers today use D-rings for hanging. They are attached to either side of the frame, with wire or twine connecting them.

• Wire is the most commonly used material for hanging; framers recommend a multistrand stainless-steel wire. Other types of wire can stretch or fail. Decorative strips of ribbon connecting more than one picture on a wall are additional hanging devices suitable for certain works. All of the paintings in Jefferson's Monticello are hung with ribbons from a brass molding so that walls are not defaced.

• Bumpers made of cork or plastic should be affixed to the back of the frame, so that the picture hangs free from the wall, allowing air circulation.

• By hanging paintings from moldings, you can avoid puncturing walls.

galleries, and framers is to leave the edges of the artwork exposed, giving a feeling of lightness to the picture. Float-matting, where the work seems to float off the mat—it is actually attached by featherweight Japanese paper hinges—also with its edges exposed, is a similar technique.

Conservators urge that four-ply 100 percent rag board always be used as matting material. The backing should be double-wall, nonacid corrugated board or plastic. Hinges should be water-soluble, preferably starch paste on Japanese paper rather than damaging adhesives. No adhesive tape—even if it is called acid-free or archival—is acceptable.

• As with paintings, insulated, waterproof, impact-resistant backing is an excellent protective material. Water is the most common threat to works on paper. If they do become wet, your first step should be to interleaf them with paper towels until the conservator can reach them. Freeze-drying is even better, but it is not available to many people. A stain such as coffee should not be rubbed or soaked, but taken to the conservator as quickly as possible.

• It is almost always advisable to place works on paper

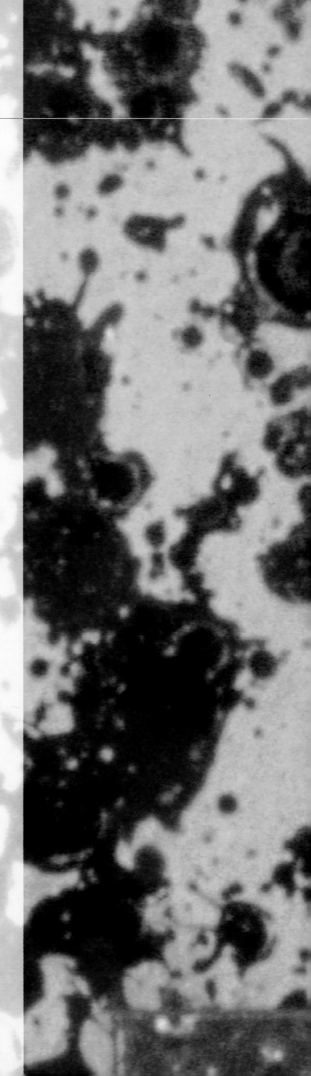

STUDY OF TWO PEARS

WALLACE STEVENS

I

Opusculum paedagogum.

The pears are not viols,

Nudes or bottles.

They resemble nothing else.

II

They are yellow forms

Composed of curves

Bulging toward the base.

They are touched red.

III

They are not flat surfaces

Having curved outlines.

They are round

Tapering toward the top.

IV

In the way they are modelled

There are bits of blue.

A hard dry leaf hangs

From the stem.

V

The yellow glistens.

It glistens with various yellows,

Citrons, oranges and greens

Flowering over the skin.

VI

The shadows of the pears

Are blobs on the green cloth.

The pears are not seen

As the observer wills.

THE WRITER'S
VISION

An entrance to a Philippine pygmy hut, a Lipchitz painting, and a
Biedermeier chest with Mayan and African sculptural pieces set the
stage for Albee's diverse art collection. On the far wall is a painting by
John McLaughlin (right) and a dramatic, black and red Michael
David opposite the African birthing bed.

EDWARD ALBEE

I DON'T CONSIDER MYSELF A COLLECTOR — IT'S PRETENTIOUS. I'M AN ACCUMULATOR.

Edward Albee greets you at the metal door that shields his art-rich loft in an old industrial neighborhood in lower Manhattan. He leads you into a freight elevator that rattles up four floors and opens onto a cavernous, dramatically underlit space. You're instantly struck with the inventive way he has made art accessible. Every surface is a backdrop for art, including the rough-grained wood floor where sculptural objects are positioned to challenge perspective. To encourage close-up view, art is placed on waist-high wall ledges, tabletops, cabinets, and bookcases throughout the room. Art becomes an intimate experience for those who settle into the couches that Albee has arranged as islands of seating to intermingle people and the African sculptures that hover close by. To get an eye-level view of the art suspended from the upper reaches of the loft, you simply climb the spiral staircase to the balcony off Albee's bedroom study. His adventurous vision of art continues when you travel out to his land's end retreat on Long Island. Here you share the excitement of his discovery of a new generation of artists.

Viewed together, Albee's TriBeCa and Montauk homes reveal his resolute pursuit of an astonishing assemblage of art: classical and contemporary, masterworks of the midcentury, first works of artists of the eighties and nineties, and a commanding presence of African

ABOVE

In the library/study, a Rand Hardy wall construction is suspended over the Eames lounge and ottoman where Albee retreats to write and read.

OVERLEAF

A Thai bed becomes a coffee table, centering a seating arrangement that intermingles Albee's friends with African tribal figures. Balancing the scene is a Dogon granary door (left) *and a wood construction by Bettina Berkle* (right). *A stark red brick wall is a backdrop for seven decades of abstract works by* (from left to right) *John Sennhauser, Arp, Kandinsky, Gallatin, Ella Bergman, and Alistair Milne.*

ceremonial and utilitarian sculptural objects. Art in both houses was hung and placed by Albee, who appreciates the symbiotic relationship that exists between the art of different eras and cultures. Paintings, prints, and drawings that he has been acquiring since the 1950s are displayed in juxtaposition to a New Guinea funeral mask, a six-hundred-year-old bowl from Central Africa, a New Guinea shield, a pre-Columbian grinding board, and a decoration from an Indian funeral cart.

"I've learned that there is a difference when someone puts together a collection themselves, believes in it, and hangs the art, as I have always done," Albee explains. "I'm not one of those people who hire someone to create a collection for them, and then call in someone to decorate the place with it. Nor do I believe you should buy art to impress people or to make money with it. You just might be better off buying a young artist whose work you think is interesting. It may be a better work of art, and you have the satisfaction of having done something important."

Albee's summer home, a fisherman's cottage transformed into a sixties modern house, looks outward to the sea, all light and open space. The work of young artists dominates here and the house is an appropriate framework for art of the moment and the future. In contrast, his cloistered TriBeCa home is a memory trip, the walls charting a time line of art discovery, celebrating his earliest acquisitions—a 1909 Chagall painting and a 1930 Kandinsky oil—as well as works that illuminate a lifelong receptivity to a sweeping range of artistic expressions. Prominent are the works of Milton Avery, Walt Kuhn, Louise Nevelson, John Duff, Elizabeth Murray, Saul Steinberg, Leonard Baskin, Pavel Tchelitchew, Charles Shaw, William Zorach, and A. E. Gallatin.

Albee doesn't consider himself a collector. "It's pretentious," he says. "I'm an accumulator. I never gave away anything I liked. I still have the very first painting I bought, and it's a very good one. It was the work of a young artist who was having his first exhibition at the New Museum

172

in Richmond, Virginia. From the beginning I trusted my own taste. Along the way I developed a strong visual sense and started looking at things differently."

Edward Albee's earliest memories of home, where he was surrounded by art from a very early age, are of walls filled with "some very good Barbizon School landscapes." Many of these were collected by his impresario grandfather to fill colossal vaudeville theaters in the twenties. "I started drawing when I was five or six, and although I wanted to be many things—a composer when I discovered Bach—I kept drawing and painting until I was sixteen. In prep school I rented reproductions of twentieth-century paintings from the Lawrenceville school library. I filled my tiny room with Kandinsky, Mondrian, and—still my favorite—van Gogh, *The Artist's Bedroom.*

"By the time I was seventeen or eighteen I was visiting MOMA and the best galleries in New York City. I can still remember the charge I felt walking up several flights to explore a museum that was breaking new art ground, the Museum of Non-Objective Painting, now the Guggenheim. It was my first exposure to Klee, Kandinsky, Léger—painters who were considered art revolutionaries."

After being thrown out of school and disinherited, Albee left home and landed flat broke in New York City at the age of twenty. It would be ten years before he wrote *The Zoo Story.* He is nostalgic about living "the

MONTAUK

A Betty Parsons painting and Padavano's iron horse rest on a pine sideboard chest in the dining room. They are reflected in the mirror along with a seated African figure.

In a kitchen vignette, Albee pairs the work of the late painter and dealer Betty Parsons with ceramicist Diane Mayo. The steel staircase leads to Albee's studio.

bohemian life" in Greenwich Village in the fifties. "Art was affordable then," he says. "It was a time when you could live simply and learn a lot just wandering about the city. I'm still doing it. For years and years I've been going to museums, galleries, and artists' studios, looking for things I like. New York is wonderful. There are fifteen galleries I trust, and they handle mostly younger artists. I enjoy taking chances and helping not only young artists but those who have been overlooked."

Although acclaimed for his devotion to the literary arts and his support for young playwrights, less is known of Albee's commitment to the visual arts. His sustained support of successive generations of artists comes alive in his Montauk home and the two great barns he restored on the tip of Long Island thirty-three years ago. "The Barn" has provided living and working space for a summer colony of more than six hundred aspiring artists, sculptors, and writers since it opened in 1966. "It occurred to me to do something useful with the money I earned from *Who's Afraid of Virginia Woolf?*" Albee explains. He established the Edward F. Albee Foundation, believing that "All arts relate to each other and we can learn from each other." As they have, according to artists-in-residence Rex Lau and Diane Mayo, who have served

as guardians of Albee's "creative persons center" for more than eighteen years. "We came out to look after the dogs in exchange for the studio for a year, but stayed on. He gave us the greatest gift you can give an artist—the time and freedom to work and the confidence to develop." Lau's paintings and Mayo's art pottery were displayed prominently in Albee's Montauk home long before they were accepted by galleries and museums.

Albee's country living room is filled with sea-reflected light and a mix of African, Asian, and western art, textiles, and objects. A serene David Craven painting hangs behind a sculpture by French artist Ossip Zadkine. Surrounding the fireplace are an African war canoe remnant (above), a sculpture by Zero Higashida (left), and Thomas's totems (right).

JOHN ASHBERY

MORE OF MY FRIENDS ARE ARTISTS THAN POETS. MUCH OF THE ART I LIVE WITH WASN'T CHOSEN BY ME.

The worlds of art and poetry converge in John Ashbery's life and homes. They illuminate his historic 1894 house in Hudson River country and his writer's lair in one of New York City's oldest neighborhoods, Chelsea. Pulitzer Prize–winning poet John Ashbery candidly admits to having been more influenced by modern painting and music than by poetry. "More of my friends are artists than poets," he says. "Much of the art I live with wasn't chosen by me; it was given to me by artists who are friends of mine or whom I have written about." In writing about one of these artists, Jane Freilicher, whose work hangs in both homes, Ashbery says, "I gravitated toward painters, probably because the particular painters I knew happened to be more fun than many of the poets."

Freilicher was the first artist Ashbery met when he moved to New York to attend Columbia graduate school in 1949. "Despite or because of our common trait of shyness," he says, "Jane and I became friends." Through her and their mutual friend, poet Kenneth Koch, he was introduced into New York's fermenting art community. Ashbery recalls "Larry Rivers, Robert de Niro, and Al

Kresch, who painted in a loose figurative style that echoed Bonnard and Matisse but with an edge of frenzy or anxiety that mimicked New York. There was Jane, whose paintings struck me at first as tentative, a quality I have since come to admire and consider one of her strengths, having concluded that most good things are tentative, or should be."

Like his poetry, the art essays Ashbery wrote for more than twenty-five years for the *International Herald Tribune* when he lived in Paris, and for *ArtNews, Newsweek,* and *New York* while in America, reveal as much about him as they do about the artists he wrote of. In his 1986 essay on Freilicher, Ashbery describes the influence abstract expressionism had on his artist friends as well as on his poetry, describing it as "a heroic period from which we all benefited. We were in awe of de Kooning, Pollock, Rothko, and Motherwell. We attended concerts of John Cage's music, Merce Cunningham's dances, and the Living Theatre. I could see all of this entering into Jane's work, Larry Rivers's, and my own." Ashbery remembers the Museum of Modern Art's shows of Munch, Matisse, Vuillard, and Soutine, whose art, in particular, "was full of

OPPOSITE

Ashbery's front parlor is a mix of styles and periods with a larger-than-life painting of a rose by his friend Alex Katz, an antique Persian Khorasson carpet, and a nineteenth-century bronze figure, a sentinel in the doorway.

Ashbery sits in his parlor where he arranged the art he most likes to look at: his portrait (left) by a longtime friend, the late Fairfield Porter, and a jarring Sue Daykin painting of a fictional political assassination attempt over the sofa.

178

possibilities for painters and poets," he says. "I began pushing my poems around and standing words on end," he wrote. "The fact that the sky could come crashing joyously onto the grass, that trees could dance upside down and houses roll over like cats to have their tummies scratched was something I hadn't realized before."

There is a very personal, idiosyncratic quality in the way Ashbery lives with art in his Hudson home. It calls to mind a description of his poetry as "the discontinuity of ideas." "I was trying to do two different things with the house," Ashbery explains. "On one hand, I wanted to decorate it the way I thought a small-town bourgeois family who had traveled overseas and picked up Piranesi prints and Japanese objects might have decorated it when it was built. But I also wanted to display the work I had accumulated, which wasn't particularly suited to the character of the house." Acknowledging a "fondness for a

polyphony of clashing styles," Ashbery arranged in the Victorian parlor the contemporary art of several of his friends. He admits, "I didn't try to preserve a mood in this room. It had more wall space, so I was able to hang more things in it that I like to look at."

In contrast, a turn-of-the-century atmosphere prevails from the elaborate glass front doors through the rest of this landmark house. Ashbery preserved the original wall covering in the dining room and, with humor, placed a portrait by an unknown artist of an unknown man over the fireplace as if it were a revered ancestor. A prized collection of Piranesi prints enriches the library. Japanese prints acquired in London in the early 1970s, "when they were cheap, twenty-five to thirty dollars," frame the staircase wall.

Three generations of one family lived in the house before Ashbery bought it in 1978, leaving behind many reminders of its historical roots. "A lot of the furniture came with the house," Ashbery says. "It was old, and the owners were leaving some of it behind." Ashbery found an attic full or memorabilia, family photographs in old picture frames, a baby's crib. The art pottery collection he has on the library mantel began with one little piece found in the basement coal bin—a much prized Grueby vase.

Ashbery has been intimately involved in all the details that distinguish his home. He has brought to it things from his parents' and grandparents' summer house on Lake Ontario. He has chosen and used everything to create a very personal environment—pillows and rugs, textiles and furniture, paintings and sculpture, and the vintage lampshades he loves and collects.

In the living hall at the bottom of the stairs hang Chinese scrolls on velvet, setting off an arrangement of Chinese Chippendale furniture.

The dining room is a paean to Alfonso Ossorio, with three walls

devoted to his surrealist paintings and assemblages. Edward Higgins's

stainless-steel sideboard, a companion piece to three massive Higgins

tables that anchor the room. Extreme right, a partial view of

Rauschenberg's first lithograph, Abby's Bird.

B.H. & ABBY FRIEDMAN

WHEN AN ARTIST BECOMES WELL KNOWN, WE LET THE ART GO AND REPLACE IT WITH THE WORK OF SOMEONE UNDISCOVERED.

They named their first child Jackson. He was born soon after Jackson Pollock died. B.H. describes it as an act of homage to a man who had a most profound influence on his thinking. "Pollock was the first artist with whom I developed a deep understanding and relationship," B.H. says. "He taught me about freedom. By exposing me to a new kind of art and aesthetic, he helped me to draw on my own feelings and experiences, liberating my life and writing."

The Friedmans met Pollock in 1955 when collector Ben Heller brought the artist and his wife, Lee Krasner, to the Friedmans' to view their collection of modern masters. In addition to a 4-by-4-foot 1949 Pollock oil, B.H. and Abby already owned three Arp sculptures, a Mondrian gouache, paintings by Feininger and Klee, and several collages by Laurens and Schwitters.

"When I started to make some money in real estate," B. H. explains, "Abby and I discovered galleries and began to buy art. Betty Parsons, Sidney Janis, and Curt Valentin let us spread out payment over time. Curt was especially important in building my art education. He would recommend books to read and talk with me about artists who were breaking new ground." B.H. remembers buying one of the Arp sculptures for $600, the Pollock and Mondrian for about $1,000 each.

In 1963, Friedman jettisoned fifteen years of a lucrative career with power builders, the Uris brothers (his uncles), to pursue his lifelong interest in writing—but not before he convinced the firm that art improves the quality of life in the workplace as well as in the home. To distinguish several major buildings in New York, B.H. commissioned murals from rising stars Alex Katz, Robert Rauschenberg, Alfonso Ossorio, Lee Krasner, and David Hare.

B.H. and Abby moved out of New York in the 1960s, choosing to live successively in Provincetown and the Hamptons. Their lives revolved around these historic art

Revealing their love of artist-designed furniture, B.H. and Abby look into a mirror by Richard Kreznar and sit at a steel Edward Higgins bar on stools by French architect/designer Pierre Chareau.

The Friedman bathroom is filled with memorabilia from artist friends. William Copley did the paintings of the Friedman children, Daisy (left) and Jackson (right).

182

communities and the friendships they made with several artists, many of whom B.H. has written about, including Franz Kline, Willem de Kooning, Alfonso Ossorio, and Jackson Pollock.

B.H. and Abby's two current homes, an apartment that looks over New York's skyline and a house that looks over Georgica Pond in East Hampton, contain a visual history of their shared commitment to living with art and their devotion to their many artist friends. Memorabilia are interspersed with inscribed artwork. Framed photographs, letters, and newspaper clippings recall gallery events, art openings, book signings, dinner parties, beach picnics, and art happenings.

The entry hall of their New York apartment is filled with art that reinforces the remembrance of good times past. Two paintings by Franz Kline, one poignantly titled *Jackson,* are grouped with a small Barnett Newman and a Pollock drawing, both gifts from the artists. Their dining room is a paean to Alfonso Ossorio, with three walls

devoted to his surrealist paintings and assemblages. Robert Rauschenberg's first lithograph, *Abby's Bird,* hangs above an Edward Higgins stainless-steel sideboard that on first view appears to be a wall sculpture. It is a companion piece to three massive Higgins tables that anchor the room.

Juxtaposed to the modern masters are paintings and furniture by several artists whom B.H. says "have not received the attention they deserve." When you enter the Friedmans' New York home, two impressive works by Martin Ramirez, "the greatest of the American Art Brut artists," capture your attention. A wall in their living room is dedicated to the works of second-generation abstract expressionists Norman Bluhm, Robert Goodnough, and Salvatore Scarpitta. Both homes exhibit the work of Rick Klauber, Fritz Bultman, and Joellen Hall, whom B.H. describes as "a visionary whose work fits in the Hamptons but is equally at home in New York."

The Friedmans no longer own the Pollock, Mondrian, or other works from their early collection. B.H. explains: "When an artist becomes very well known, it's important that we let the art go and replace it with the work of someone undiscovered, unappreciated, or young."

Abby counters, "That is the difference between Bobby and me. I don't need to have anything, but once we get it, it is very hard to let go."

Works by known and lesser known artists mingle on the walls of the Friedman entrance hall. Above the Nico Yektai bench are two Art Brut works by Martin Ramirez and a cluster of small works on paper by master artists—two Franz Klines, a Jackson Pollock, and a Barnett Newman.

Above a backgammon table made by Edward Higgins is a 1953 wrapped piece by Salvatore Scarpitta. In a recessed wall space created for art is a painting by second generation abstract expressionist Norman Bluhm, and a corner dedicated to Joseph Cornell collages.

There has been a conscious effort to establish a stylistic difference in each of the Friedman homes. B.H. points out that "We have abstract art in New York and mostly figurative art in the Hamptons." However, the mood they create in each is similar—one of order and tranquillity. Rather than crowd his art, B.H. had three windows in the New York living room blocked out to create more wall space.

"With the exception of some gifts, everything you see in our homes Abby and I selected together," B.H. says. "If I don't like something that Abby likes, we don't get it, and vice versa. The same system of checks and balances takes place now that we are commissioning art furniture for our New York apartment." In contrast to the Stickley furniture that is so appropriate for their country house, their New York apartment is starkly beautiful because of the sculptured steel furniture that artist Edward Higgins made for them. B.H. remembers Abby questioning the design for the top of a coffee table, which she saw as a cross, feeling it was unsuitable for a Jewish home. "Higgins and I persuaded her to go along." B.H. says, "and she never regretted it."

JOE LeSUEUR

I MIX UP ARTISTS WHO ARE KNOWN AND NOT SO WELL KNOWN. IT'S LESS SNOBBISH, MORE DEMOCRATIC.

On first meeting, Joe LeSueur tells you he's conflicted. "My place is small. I'm always wrestling with the space I need for books and the space I want to give art." During his career as an editor and writer, LeSueur built a sizable library and an equally formidable collection of paintings, prints, and photographs. "I can't have my books up high," he tells you, "because then there would be no room for the art that I love living with."

At the suggestion of a writer friend, LeSueur added a cozy wing for himself onto her eighteenth-century Hamptons house in 1985. He made the decision when he moved in that every wall in every room would become a showcase for the more than one hundred pieces of art he had acquired over thirty years. This decision required that LeSueur approach each wall as a book designer does when he creates a layout.

"I think I have a good eye when it comes to knowing how to hang pictures," he says. "I do it myself, and it's fun. I've seen many collections where the works fight with each other, so I do everything to avoid this. When paintings are well installed, they look better in someone's

house than they do in a gallery because you can create contrasts and patterns." He tells you this as he points to a wall that is totally devoted to Joan Mitchell's abstract pastels and explains that he deliberately faced them with a wall of Joe Brainard's figurative paintings, collages, and drawings to create a dramatic counterpoint. "Pictures can be in contrast but not in conflict," he explains, "so that's why, when I get a new painting, I move everything around. I enjoy creating a new atmosphere, not only for me but for my friends who like to hear why I've done what I've done. When you keep things in the same place year after year, you don't see them anymore." LeSueur often reframes his art for the same reason.

He is equally clear about preferring to under-light his art. He is opposed to elaborate lighting systems because he likes to see art during the day in natural light. "At night," he continues, "it's nice to make an effort to see a painting and to discover it." That is the explanation he gives for once positioning a Duchamp work on paper that he says is "worth a lot" in an out-of-the-way hallway. "I liked the idea of people being surprised when they came upon it."

OPPOSITE

Joe LeSueur relaxes in his garden living room where he has massed a wide-ranging collection by known as well as young and local artists. He admires a dense arrangement of works by artist friends: Rudy Burckhardt, de Kooning, Robert Harms, Duchamp, Paul Thek, and Jasper Johns.

The art in LeSueur's house is an eclectic mix of gifts from artist friends and works he bought with what he calls his sinking fund, a banking term describing a fund set up to pay off debts. "The difference is," he says, "my fund is all for art." LeSueur started the fund when he sold one of the many paintings his good friend Joan Mitchell had given him. He remembers her admonishing him, "If you ever need money, sell it, but wait until it's worth

Above the sofa is a painting by John Button of a woman LeSueur knows, which adds to his enjoyment of the picture. Emma Rivers made a coffee table collage out of Matisse postcards LeSueur brought back from the Hermitage.

something." In the 1980s when the market was booming, LeSueur asked a dealer to look at a very large Joan Mitchell painting; "I told her I wanted $250,000 for it, and she said she'd have it sold by tomorrow. The capital

CHARLES & SANDRA HOBSON

ART IS A KEY TO UNLOCK THE SPIRIT.

For some people, art is so much a part of their lives that it seeps into every career or activity they embark upon. Charles Hobson was a lawyer who loved to paint, and his wife was a working artist. At the age of forty, Charles gave up the law, entered the San Francisco Art Institute, and took a degree in printmaking. With his newfound skills, he then put together a book about a friend who had died. This experience turned him in the direction of making artists' books, which he now does full-time, using both his own work and that of artist friends. Meanwhile Sandra, with little time for painting while raising their two children, maintained her connection to art by becoming a docent at San Francisco's Museum of Modern Art and, later, president of the board.

Early in their marriage, the Hobsons started to collect the work of Bay Area artists. They acquired paintings seriously for about ten years, buying the work of young artists. "We got to know them; they became part of our lives," Sandra recalls. "It was a learning process." The Hobsons' first passion was ceramics and sculpture, but they moved on to figurative paintings and works on paper, setting aside a percentage of their income to make purchases, either individually or jointly. "We'd go to all the openings, gradually refining our interests and tastes," Sandra explains. "The more art you see, the more you develop an aesthetic."

Fourteen years ago they bought the house they now live in, a splendid nineteenth-century home with dark wood moldings, long corridors, and a fine central staircase. They fell in love with the house even though it is not the perfect place in which to display art. The rooms are not particularly large, the moldings, while an important aspect of the architecture, severely limit the wall space, and there are no gallery-like open areas such as one often finds in contemporary houses and apartments. The house had the right feeling as a family home, however, and they never regretted their choice.

"Just after we moved in, Chuck bought me a painting by Oliver Jackson that measured 107 by 117 inches," Sandra remembers. "Four men had to carry it upstairs. But it was simply too big for the house, and we donated it to the Fine Arts Museum." Clearly, the Hobsons do not buy a painting with any plan as to where it is

OPPOSITE

Within the strong architectural framework of this house, Charles Hobson's double portrait of Henry Miller and Anaïs Nin over the mantelpiece creates the focal point of the living room. The ceramic figure at right is by Robert Brady.

190

The Hobsons' bedroom, a serene retreat with muted colors and simple furnishings, features a nature-loving bed by Agnes Bourne. The big painting on the far wall is by Tom Lieber. The arrow over the bed is by Deborah Orapallo.

going to hang. "We'll come home with something and have to move everything else around. But that's always a good experience. Rehanging the art is like acquiring a whole new collection."

In recent years they have been buying less, giving away more, and focusing on artists' books. Charles Hobson, whose work has been exhibited in many museums, makes his elegant creations in the basement studio of the house. The books have mostly literary or historical themes—for example, *Parisian Encounters,* a ring-bound book about meetings in Paris between people like George Sand and Frédéric Chopin, Napoleon and Josephine, and Anaïs Nin and Henry Miller. The book contains fragments of their writings, their portraits, and

maps of Paris where they met. (Since the pages flip out, the reader can change the order and have, for instance, Napoleon facing off against Anaïs Nin!)

But if the Hobsons have slowed down on their acquisition of paintings in favor of books, they remain friends with many artists, and still meet new ones, from whom they gather inspiration. "We are very process-oriented," Charles says. "We love the dialogue that occurs between artists and those who look at art."

At the far end of the kitchen a carved female figure by John Buck stands beside four paintings by Squeak Carnwath. The candlestick figure on the counter is by Carl Dern. The photograph near the pillar is by the Hobsons' daughter, Mary Daniel Hobson.

Perhaps it is not surprising, given this delight in the interaction of artist and art lover, that Sandra Hobson has now given up her museum career to become a counselor with a group that uses art as a healing force. "It's not therapy," she explains. "It's community outreach—people making art to heal themselves, their communities, and their environment. For me, art is not just about visual communication. It's an access point to something deeper. Art is a key to unlock the spirit."

MARIE-FRANCE POCHNA

THEY ARE MY MADELEINES. THEY BRING BACK MEMORIES.

Just as Frenchwomen can put together a look, seemingly effortlessly, with just a scarf or a wrap, so writer Marie-France Pochna has created a serene and congenial look in her Paris apartment with very little money, by mixing the furniture and fabrics she likes with her inexpensive finds and personal gifts of art.

"I grew up with mainly good-quality antiques that seemed to go along with good food and good conversation," Marie-France recalls. That decor resulted in "an unpretentious atmosphere. I owe my love of painting to being taken to the Louvre. I must have been about seven or eight, and I still remember the shock when I first discovered Vermeer. Here was an interior world that appealed to my imagination." So appealing in fact, that she started collecting postcards of the art she loved.

In 1965, she traveled to the United States, where she met artists involved in abstract expressionism and visited Kenneth Noland and Jules Olitski in Vermont. From then on, she spent a lot of time in the art world, particularly with gallery owner Alexandre Iolas, who was a close friend of Dominique de Menil and contributed to her

collection. Marie-France's modest budget limited her purchases, but she loves the work of the French artists Arman and César, and she owns several small bronzes by both. "They are my madeleines," she says. "They bring back memories."

Another friend is the American artist Tom Wesselmann, who persuaded her to pose nude for one of his bedroom series. She was very nervous about agreeing to such a request, but an artist's proof of the edition, one of his most subtle and elegant, now hangs in her bedroom, his gift to her.

Marie-France, an attorney, gave up the law to be with her then-husband whose business took him to Saudi Arabia and Egypt. On her return to France, she decided to write. Her first biography, of Marcel Boussac, made her name. Since then she has written biographies of Gianni Agnelli, Nina Ricci, and Christian Dior, and is currently working on a book about Bernard Arnault and the story of LVMH (Louis Vuitton Moët Hennessy), the conglomerate that includes Dior, Givenchy, Lacroix, and Kenzo.

The two-bedroom apartment near the Place des Victoires, where she lives and works, was once part of a larger one that belonged to her grandmother. Marie-France made few structural changes when she moved here in 1987, but it is her own belongings that mark the place immediately as her own. Every part of the apartment attests to her friendships with artists in France and

OPPOSITE

Marie-France Pochna's salon is a hymn to the muted grays and greens of Paris, the City of Light. The large screen, commissioned by her from American artist David Webster, breaks up the book-lined wall at the far end of the room.

ABOVE

The entranceway to this Paris apartment is hung with two nineteenth-century Grisaille panels, one of which is reflected in a mirror. Two Chinese vases sit on a table at the far end, along with a small sculpture by César. The large vase is from the 1930s.

LEFT

In a spotlit niche in her bookshelves, Marie-France displays her collection of 1930s glass, some bought, others inherited. They include Dinanderies glass and vases by Gallé.

A wall Marie-France looks at when she is in bed displays her portrait by Tom Wesselmann on the left, a canvas by Yves Lévêque (a good friend) in the middle, and on the right another Wesselmann.

in the United States. Perhaps the most striking piece is the screen at one end of the salon. Like most writers, Marie-France has a large library. "I wanted to break the bookish look of the room," she says. An admirer of American artist David Webster, who lived in Paris for twenty-two years, she asked him to make her a screen. "I like his assimilation of painting and sculpture in the same work and the way he transforms objects with a Dadaist kind of humor." The screen that Webster designed provides the clue to her writing life. Its four gray-to-ocher panels trace the metamorphosis of wood into paper and into its final stage, the book. The screen also dominates one of the book-lined walls, just as Marie-France had hoped.

Although her art collection is eclectic, there is a 1930s flavor to the apartment. She has furniture by Josef Hoffmann, Gallé glass, Viennese textiles, and an overall decorative style reminiscent of Eileen Gray. But perhaps in the end what the visitor finds most affecting about this writer's lair is the color palette of all the works of art. Mostly gray, gray-blue, and soft ocher, they are essentially the shades of Paris. "Christian Dior once said that fashion originated in Paris because it inscribed itself naturally in its monuments, along its river, and in the harmony of the architecture," she says. "I would add the skies. In Paris the skies are constantly changing. I love the city's infinite variety from pink to gray—the rooftops, the architecture, the misty light, and above all, the sky—*le ciel de Paris.*"

THE ART
OF THE HANG

HOW TO HANG
AND DISPLAY ART

So you've brought home your treasured artwork. It's framed just the way you want it. Now you need to hang it on the wall. But which wall? A blank wall? A wallpapered wall? High on the wall? In the middle of the wall? With a lot of other pictures or by itself? Suddenly questions start raining down, and that thrilling moment of hanging your picture rapidly dissipates into creative confusion.

Alec Cobbe, artist and independent consultant, most frequently to the National Trust art collections in Britain, has spent most of his life hanging the pictures that belong either to his own family or to the collections of the National Trust, one of which is exhibited (and open to

Sometimes an uncluttered look with a pale color for a background works best for art, as in art patron Ann Hatch's bedroom in San Francisco. The paintings are by Raphael Soyer (right) and Alfred Maurer (left).

the public) at Hatchlands, in Surrey, where he lives and works (see Directory).

Cobbe explains that it was considered normal in Elizabethan and Georgian houses and in collectors' private galleries of those periods, which customarily had very high ceilings, to hang pictures densely, packing the wall space three or even four tiers high. The most important pictures were always hung low enough to be easily seen by the viewer; the lesser works were placed way up high. Continental and American houses of those periods also followed this method. Artists in the eighteenth and nineteenth centuries respected this convention and, anticipating the hang, as it is called, often worked to achieve an interaction between one painting and another. "Pictures are gregarious animals," Cobbe says. "This interaction between paintings often enhanced those around them."

The great early American collectors, such as Andrew Mellon, J. P. Morgan, H. E. Huntington, and Henry Clay Frick, followed this tradition when they brought home their old master paintings, mostly purchased in Europe, to display in their fine mansions. But density fell out of fashion after 1920. People began to think that the artworks suffered from these visual cocktail parties, and by the middle of the twentieth century, in reaction to what was thought of as Victorian clutter, walls were stripped and pictures were required to hang in isolation amid vast amounts of empty space. Modern art tended to respond to this spatial revolution, and now museum galleries are required to be bigger and bigger to accommodate ever-larger canvases.

At the same time, however, twentieth-century architects greatly reduced the height of ceilings in most new homes, so the practice of double or triple rows of paintings became impossible. The late Suzanne Railey experienced this firsthand when she moved with her extensive art collection from her apartment in Paris, which had 24-foot ceilings, to one in New York with 9½-foot ceilings. Her solution? She mirrored the ceilings, which gave height to the rooms and provided breathing space for the pictures.

196

LEFT

The wall in one of the grand salons of Harewood House, Yorkshire, is a perfect example of the traditional hang (produced by Alec Cobbe), with dark red background, paintings hung in tiers up to the moldings, each lit with overframe lights.

BELOW

These master drawings by Friedrich, Tiepolo, Redon, and Delacroix (all from the Thaws' collection) are enriched by an elegant fabric wall covering by Liberty of London.

197

The preferred background for art has also changed with the times. In earlier centuries, red was the most commonly used wallpaper or paint color to set off the pictures. A soft warm ruby color enhanced the gilded frames and rich oil paintings of the past. Most experts believe the most common mistake people make today, however, is to use too light or bright a background behind a painting. Anything that distracts the eye from the work is to be avoided.

Siting indoor sculpture demands different conditions. Depending on its size and the size of the pedestal, you should take into account how the piece will work in a room and how the light sources will be directed. Sculptor Juan Muñoz suggests that the space given to sculpture is like a clearing in the forest: "You are not really in the forest, but you are surrounded by trees."

Today, as attitudes change, so do hanging styles. Many museums have completely rehung their works. With the new thinking about displaying art, as art critic John Russell says, "installation has become a subdepartment of sociability, in which paintings, drawings, and photographs come out into the room to greet us."

That is perhaps the goal of all art-hangers: to have the artworks come out into the room to greet us. Sometimes people buy a picture and know precisely where it will hang in order to offer such a greeting. But for those who are doubtful, here are some guidelines:

Paintings

• Decide which room to hang your picture in. Then study the room's size and architectural details. "You can't ignore the volumes, the dimensions," Alec Cobbe says. In a small room, a huge canvas may be difficult to see properly. In a big room, a delicate drawing might get lost. Try to establish a good fit.

• Put your best pictures in prominent places and group the others so they benefit. "Quality, size, and subject matter are all important," Alec Cobbe believes. "It's no use having an ideal hang in mind, then lamenting that the collection doesn't fit your plan. The art comes first."

• Examine other people's walls, and study the displays in art museums. Do you like clutter, symmetry, or simplicity? That is a question of your own personal taste.

• Study the visual qualities of your artwork. If it is pale in color, a dark background might enhance its subtlety. If it is bright, a muted wall treatment might be preferable. If it is complex in design, a busy wallpaper or fabric might be visually confusing, whereas a stark image can shine against a patterned background. A rule of thumb from Alec Cobbe: the background color should *never* be brighter than the brightest color in the picture. But don't hesitate to experiment. As designer Sally Sirkin Lewis says, "People often think that everything needs to be neutral to enhance art, but that's not true." She suggests that the contrast of black-and-white prints, photographs, or a Franz Kline next to a red sofa or walls of primary colors can be very effective.

In the stairwell of design consultant Geraldine Stutz's New York duplex, views of English country houses, Venetian facades, and botanicals.

• Many art lovers like to hang pictures together to increase their impact if they are in the same style, from the same period, or of the same subject. Leave breathing-space between them, though; otherwise the images might interfere with each other. Alec Cobbe likes to see them hung "like postage stamps," as was done in the eighteenth and nineteenth centuries.

• If you are planning to "do a hang," try laying out your artworks on the floor and rearranging them until you like the result before you put the nails in the wall. "There is no one correct way the pieces go together," says David Kassel, founder of Freelance Art Services (see Directory). "You can't see it till you see it."

• If you hang a row of pictures horizontally, even if they are all different sizes, either line up the top or bottom of each frame, or leave them all uneven. Be consistent in your geometrical plan.

• When you hang a single picture, a general rule is to place it at eye level. In a living room or dining room, for instance, where people may look at the art while sitting down, you might lower the hanging level.

• Hanging artworks on a staircase wall is an efficient use of display space, particularly for detailed works such as photographs, which can be examined at close quarters as the visitor climbs or descends.

• A new display idea is to prop your pictures up on a ledge or shelf. "People like ledges," says Randy Bourne, the founder and president of Exposures, a catalog for framing and hanging photographs, "because you can constantly change your art without putting holes in the wall." As other ledge fans point out, you can also display many more pictures in this way, stacked behind each other.

Sculpture

• Most sculpture requires a pedestal or base of some kind. Sculptors often recommend the form of display they prefer for their work. Galleries and museums are also good reference points.

• Sculpture should not be placed where it is easy to stumble over. There should be space to walk around it, so every dimension may be admired. "Sometimes a piece will even turn its back on the viewer," says sculptor Cristina Iglesias.

• It is useful to think of sculpture in relation to the furniture in the room, as both are three-dimensional and have specific functions, whether passive or active. It is a good idea to place the sculpture in some kind of perspective or vista, so that the eye can be easily led to the work of art. The use of mirrors can be effective in enhancing the three-dimensional effect.

• Make sure the lighting will illuminate the work in a way that enhances its contours.

• Displaying small sculptures on a mantel or shelf can often increase their impact.

The Environment

The environment in which you display your artwork will have a major effect on its survival. The work can suffer from inappropriate climate conditions, which may cause flaking, molding, or buckling. Also, canvas, wood, and Masonite, frequently used for frames or supports, may suffer from extreme climate abuse.

Regulated temperature and humidity and a steady, unfluctuating climate will prevent pictures from drying out or becoming moldy. Try to keep the humidity between 40 and 60 percent, and aim for a temperature within the 68- to 70-degree range.

Most homeowners can maintain these levels with air conditioners, humidifiers, dehumidifiers, and strategic hanging. In very damp climates, ceiling or floor fans can be used to maintain a regular flow of air, reducing the possibility of foxing (mottled brown spots caused by mold). Even a well-framed watercolor or pastel can suffer from foxing, because the materials in the paint and pastels respond to high heat and humidity. If foxing occurs, the artwork should be unframed immediately and aired. Mold cannot survive in less than 65 percent relative humidity.

Conservators suggest four practical rules about where to hang a picture:

• *Don't* hang a valuable picture over a working fireplace unless smoke and soot are carefully controlled.

• *Don't* place an artwork directly over a heat source such as a radiator, near a light, or next to a climate-control appliance such as an air conditioner.

• *Do* hang your artwork away from direct sunlight.

• *Don't* hang your artwork on an exterior wall where it will be affected by radical changes in the outdoor temperature.

These are conservators' guidelines; whether or not you decide to follow them to the letter will depend on the value and rarity of your pictures.

One last caveat: Alec Cobbe says that by far the most damaging thing to do to an artwork is to consign it to the attic or basement, where throughout the year temperatures and humidity fluctuate greatly.

POEM IN WHICH A PAINTING
BECOMES A POEM

for Max Gimblett

JOHN YAU

One cannot step into this river

smooth stone in which a fish swims

toward sky or molten gold

worn by clouds parting above a lake

One cannot dive into this stone

in which a fish swims toward moon

imbedded in clouds rubbed smooth

by hands polishing mirror

floating to surface of a reflection

you can hold in your hands

One cannot swim in this reflection

in which a fish swims toward surface inside moon

in which a fish swims through molten gold

worn by clouds rising behind smooth stone

PICTURE-PERFECT
SPACES

JOHN & FRANCES BOWES

SINCE WE ARE CONCENTRATING ON MINIMALISM AND ABSTRACTION, WE REALLY NEED THE SPACE.

Art comes in all shapes and sizes. A Japanese print? Hanging space no problem. An English watercolor? An easy fit. A photograph? There's always room. But what about a canvas by Robert Ryman? How do you squeeze one of Ellsworth Kelly's earlier works into your normal-size living room?

Frances and John Bowes, premier collectors of contemporary art on the West Coast, have done the only thing possible to give their paintings the space they deserve: they commissioned an architect to design a house around their works of art. The result is that not only do the paintings now communicate a unique sense of power, but the house itself, designed for the paintings, turns out to be a work of art, too.

The Boweses bought the property, on a Sonoma hillside, in 1989. That fall the architect Ricardo Legoretta started the design, and four years later the house was complete. Born and brought up in Mexico, Legoretta was influenced by his friend and mentor, Luis Barragán, and uses the flat planes of walls to create geometric shapes, almost like abstract sculpture. This particular visual aesthetic was ideal for the Boweses. "We told him we wanted a large gallery around a courtyard," John Bowes recalls, "and white walls so that the art would stand out. The dimensions, of course, had to be ample."

And so they are. The living room is 30 by 40 feet, with 16-foot ceilings, but although the dimensions are so big, the proportions ensure that one never feels overwhelmed. The courtyard, as requested, is surrounded on three sides by gallery-like corridors, where paintings and long, narrow windows compete elegantly with each other.

203

The fourth side of the courtyard opens out to a dark-tinted pool and a spectacular view of the Sonoma hills.

The enclosure is reminiscent of the walled courtyards of Chinese and Mexican houses, only here the walls and doors are made of glass, so while there is privacy, there is also a strong awareness of the outdoors. The floors are of the same materials—concrete and wood—both inside and out, reinforcing the indoor-outdoor spatial flow. All of the living quarters, including two guest rooms for the Boweses three children and eight grandchildren, are on the ground floor, so the space feels friendly.

As for the art, it all seems perfectly at home, whether in the glass-lined corridor galleries or inside the rooms. Being able to examine the canvases from a distance is a luxury usually found only in museums. "Since we are concentrating on minimalism and abstraction," Frances explains, "we really need the space."

In choosing the decor, the Boweses consulted the late interior designer Chessy Rayner. To harmonize with the Sonoma landscape, they chose Indian textiles and earth tones for the furnishings. Also, since the pictures often get changed around, a neutral background was essential. In this house, comfortably and simply decorated, the canvases sing.

John Bowes, a successful entrepreneur who was always interested in art, remarked early in their marriage that it would be fun to buy a painting. They went to a gallery in Carmel and bought a picture of the Brussels Flower Fair for $150. Gradually they became more involved. They took courses, talked to curators, traveled around the world visiting galleries and museums. They never hesitated to ask advice from experts before making a purchase.

The Boweses collect mostly in harmony, although in conversation little differences emerge:

John: We were at an auction, and Frances wanted the Susan Rothenberg that now hangs over the fireplace. I wasn't sure, thinking we might save the money for something else. Frances seized the paddle from my hand and swatted me on the head with it, knocking my glasses off—and got the painting!

Frances: I'm the impulsive one. I'll go out on a limb with young artists and photographers.

John: She goes off on her own. There's a whole floor of her purchases in our house in San Francisco. None have been allowed upstairs yet!

Frances: There was one I loved, and it went into the living room.

John: It lasted a week and a half.

These are small issues, overshadowed by their shared passion. Both are driven by the true single-mindedness of the art lover, and they talk as one about works they yearn for. "I'm dying for a Warhol," says Frances. "I'd also love an early Richter realist work."

"If the right Judd came along . . ." sighs John. His eyes light up as he talks about another favorite, Brice Marden. They like to meet the artists they admire. Good artists are very smart, John says. "Richard Serra could talk for an hour and mesmerize you."

They also enjoy hanging their paintings, although it is a challenge. "When we first got married, John hung all our pictures. He's quite tall. We have been lowering them ever since." John is always the first to ask where something will hang. "He is very interested in design, and has a wonderful eye for packaging," his wife says. "He likes to see the whole picture." There were too many paintings up and down the hall, for instance. "It spoiled the architecture." The extra paintings were hung elsewhere.

They agree that art they don't really love pulls down the other art. "We are constantly upgrading," Frances says. As they become more selective, their house continues to respond, its light-filled corridors and courtyard a constant invitation to enjoy this melding of architecture, furnishings, and art.

TOP

In the outer hall, the wrought-iron Mizner gates and colorful rug set off a 1900s Grasset poster on the far wall, a Vietnamese watercolor, and wood sculptures found in a flea market.

ABOVE

Francis Bacon and Jim Dine mark the entrance to the living room, with David Hockney's portrait of Celia at the far end. On the floor, an African lion stands guard.

The long gallerylike space of the Berlinds' apartment, with its soft

colors and furnishings, leads the eye directly to the treasures within. A

Picasso bird commands attention; a Matisse hangs over a Wendell

Castle table and a Gallé lamp.

ROGER & BROOK BERLIND

HERE WE CAN SEE THE PAINTINGS
IN A DIFFERENT WAY.

Roger Berlind spends much of his time in the mysterious depths of the theater, watching actors and actresses perform in comedies, tragedies, musicals, one-act dramas, readings. His career depends upon these theatrical experiences, for he must decide which, if any, he will produce for the American stage. Some of his successes are huge: *City of Angels, Guys and Dolls, Lettice and Lovage, Skylight, Amadeus, Sophisticated Ladies, A Funny Thing Happened on the Way to the Forum*. But it's a risky business at the best of times, full of doubt and uncertainty. Indeed it could be said that he spends much of his working life—both literally and metaphorically—in the dark.

How right it seems, therefore, that after these days and nights of intense interior life, he comes home to a wide-open space filled with light and air, punctuated by beautiful furniture and a dazzling display of a few flawless works of art.

About four years ago, the Berlinds moved from an eighth-floor apartment to the penthouse in the same New York building. They chose Henry Smith-Miller and Laurie Hawkinson to completely redesign their new home. "We'd never lived in a contemporary space before," Roger says. "They said what a wonderful opportunity it would be to combine old and new." After the new apartment was gutted, the departure point for the design was hanging the Balthus portrait of a young girl on the central wall in the living room. Colors and furniture evolved from the placement of that picture.

In an open-space theater like this, the pictures express such personality and are hung with such precision that they seem like characters from one of the plays Roger Berlind produces. "The old apartment was more compartmentalized," he says. "Here we have fewer but larger

The extraordinary portrait of a young girl by Balthus was the inspiration for all the colors and furnishings in the apartment.

rooms, creating more distance. Thus we can see the paintings in a different way." It must have been difficult—and a lot of fun—to get the staging right. "We love hanging the pictures," Brook agrees. "Roger goes around with his hammer and nails and puts them up. If you were to look behind some of them, you'd see a wall that looks like Swiss cheese."

With huge windows running the length of one side of the apartment, the light is a character in its own right. The Berlinds have installed special double shades, made of commercial blackout material, to block out sun so that a soft natural light throughout the apartment washes the pictures in a pale glow. At night warm globe bulbs set into the ceiling provide a more diffuse light than track lighting. "We don't like lights over the pictures," they explain. "That's like saying, 'Look at what we have.'" The Berlinds don't need to say it. The pictures, with their simple, direct impact on the viewer, speak for themselves.

The collection started slowly. In fact, Roger and Brook do not call themselves collectors. "I don't feel acquisitive," Roger says. "I'm not a collector in that sense. We're just feathering our nest." But feathering their nest

214

Hanging on a corridor wall are posters of some of Roger Berlind's theater productions. Roger has modestly proposed that the posters should be taken down and the space used for paintings, but Brook says "No!"

A drawing by Balthus hangs over two amusing chairs designed by the '40s French furniture designer, René Prou.

has taken on a particular aspect—the accumulation of a handful of works of art that not only are pleasing but are of exceptional quality as well. In a way, the Berlinds' apartment is like a miniature Frick Collection—rooms offering a carefully chosen selection of paintings, each one a perfect example of the artist's work.

This standard of excellence evolved from a simple seed. "My brother Robert is a professional painter," Roger explains. "He is also a great teacher and writer. Robert was helpful in making me see paintings. In my twenties and thirties he took me to museums and galleries and seduced me into loving art."

The first painting Roger Berlind bought was by Jane Freilicher, a friend of Robert's. After Roger's marriage, he and Brook began buying from dealer Vivian Horan, a good friend. The first painting the couple bought from her was a little Diebenkorn collage. Gradually, the Berlinds got hooked. "We both liked Matisse a lot, particularly the drawings," recalls Roger of their early purchases. "We also loved Picasso, Giacometti, and Balthus."

So they watched and waited, and when something wonderful came up, either through a dealer or in a

In a departure for the Berlinds, a canvas by Sean Scully resonates in the hall. The stone and wrought-iron console is by Edgar Brant. Roger Berlind works at his desk under another Scully.

gallery, they bought it. Agreement between them came easily. They prefer twentieth-century artists but exclude for the most part contemporary works. Occasionally, however, selectivity gives way to a new direction. "I wandered into a gallery fifteen years ago," Roger remembers, "and saw this black-and-white painting by Sean Scully. I'd never heard of him, but I fell in love with it." That is the familiar tale of the genuine art lover. Now he owns two Scullys and is delighted with them both.

While the taste of husband and wife almost always dovetails, there are some exceptions. Roger, for instance, loves Lucian Freud. "He would love to have a Lucian Freud," Brook says. "But I cannot live with Lucian Freud." They also returned a little Calder stabile that Brook loved because it was charming and whimsical. "Roger doesn't like charming and whimsical," she sighs.

When an acquisition fails to please, art collectors frequently return it to the dealer in exchange for something else. With the Berlinds, who are more likely to fall in love with a purchase and remain faithful, this procedure takes place only rarely. "Everything we own is on the wall," Brook says. "Nothing is in storage. We really live with our art."

A careful look at the apartment makes this clear. There is hardly anywhere to put a new painting that would not spoil the rhythm and elegance of the current arrangement. Their most recent acquisition is not a painting but a piece of sculpture, which does not take up wall space. It is a Picasso bird, bought about a year ago. "Anything we bought now would mean we'd have to give up something else," Brook explains. "And I can't imagine parting with anything. We only have one spot left, over a console in the entrance hall, and of course if we found the perfect thing . . ."

Fran pairs Donald Baechler's postmodern Rotate in Void *(1984)*
with a great furniture classic from the '50s, Eero Saarinen's womb chair
and ottoman. The spectral figure is a C. Federicki bronze sculpture.
Through the doorway are a Jonathan Silver head and a Thorton Willis
abstract painting.

CONTEMPORARY ART EXCITES ME BECAUSE IT'S ALL ABOUT IDEAS AND ABOUT THE PROVOCATIVE MATERIALS ARTISTS ARE USING TODAY.

Soon after Fran Ruwitch greets you at the front door, she draws you into her dining room and gets down on her hands and knees to plug in Tony Oursler's video sculpture, *So Blue,* which she has tucked away in a corner as a surprise. As she turns on a projector, a small cloth doll in a tacky suitcase emits baleful cries. "It's an important piece," Fran explains, "because it's bizarre and expresses the angst of our times. People seeing this fifty years from now will understand the anxiety of today." She's amused and pleased that it has become one of her husband's favorite pieces, explaining that he has not totally accepted the edgy contemporary art that she has been acquiring for fifteen years. "Lee has always been an Andrew Wyeth man who knows what he likes and likes what he knows." Fran sees Lee's growing acceptance and enjoyment of the art she has collected as evidence that "living with good art is learning about art. Now when we visit someone who has traditional art, Lee will comment that it's not very exciting."

Neither Fran nor Lee grew up with art, and for a long time they didn't think they'd be able to have any in their home because they had such different tastes and attitudes about it. However, the turning point came when Fran made a trip to the Chicago Art Expo in 1983 with veteran art collector Martin Margulies. He had been guiding her to art fairs in the United States and Europe, and she was developing a fascination for what she describes as "art

of the now." For a long time she didn't have the courage to buy anything, but on that trip she bought their first painting from an artist who was unknown at the time, Donald Baechler. "His *Rotate in Void* was so huge that there was no way to bring it into the house quietly and introduce it to Lee," Fran recalls. "I told him about it and showed him a slide, but he couldn't visualize it. When it arrived, it was overpowering for him, but now he loves it and misses it when it's borrowed for an exhibition."

Hearing this, Lee remarks, "Fran's a strong-willed person. Oftentimes when she buys something, I'm

Stephen Mueller's exuberant The Old Dorje New Bell *enlivens the family room wall leading to an open kitchen where Fran and Lee stand in front of a papier mâché and iron sculpture by Juan Munoz of a man performing acrobatics over the kitchen sink.*

217

shocked at first and protest. But as I live with the piece and get to know it, I grow to love it."

Fran positioned the forceful Baechler painting on the most prominent wall in the living room, replacing a much-loved patchwork quilt made by her mother, Eunice Cheney. It was a decision that marked a new aesthetic vision of herself and her home. "The Baechler is such a

One of Lee's favorite artworks, a Deborah Butterfield horse, is silhouetted against glass doors in the living room. On the wall behind the sofa are (left to right) a painting by Dennis Ashbaum, a neo-expressionist canvas by Wesley Kimler, and Maurizio Pellegrin's five wrapped inner tubes and photograph. An Osami Tanaka sculptural piece occupies a Mies van der Rohe coffee table.

special painting that it set a standard and influenced everything I've bought since. As soon as I put something near the Baechler that didn't match it in quality, it became immediately obvious." Fran remembers the struggle she had to find something that "would live" opposite the Baechler in their living room. "I tried a Oscar Lakeman painting there for a while, but it wasn't until I found Stephen Mueller's luminous *The Old Dorje New Bell* two years ago that I felt I had it right. They're perfect together."

The Ruwitches' cloistered, dazzling white 1960s home in southern Florida looks forward and looks back. Fran has integrated the 1950s Knoll furniture she bought when she and Lee were married forty years ago, with her

ABOVE

A painting by Henning greets guests as they come in the front door and pass by a George Segal bust relief. In front of the shuttered windows is an Osami Tanaka mixed media piece and a stacked sculpture by Emil Lukas. In the dining room, Michael David's Poppies & Remembrance II *hangs above a table surrounded by Mies van der Rohe chairs.*

ABOVE, RIGHT

Above a Florence Knoll credenza is Supplemental Reality *(1995) by Jonathan Lasker, one of Fran's favorite artists. "I'm a new me every day when I wake up and see it," she says. Richard Pousette-Dart's* Transcendental Landscape #2 *(1981–3) brings vibrancy to their minimalist bed.*

later-in-life discovery of art from the 1980s and 1990s. "Although the art and furniture evoke different periods, I think they work together," Fran says, pointing out the "silicon green and cotton candy pink" Jonathan Lasker painting that she has placed over a sleek black Florence Knoll credenza in her bedroom. "I'm essentially a minimalist, and fortunately the clean lines and sculptural quality of the furniture I've always liked don't conflict with the demanding art that I'm now committed to.

"Contemporary art excites me because it's all about ideas and about the provocative materials artists are using today," Fran says, leading a visitor to her newest acquisition, which is waiting to be hung. It's Peter Halley's *First Strike,* a painting that reverberates with Day-Glo and metallic paint. A sculpture made of found objects bound with wire spelling out the word "Transformed" is mounted on the ceiling in a hallway that leads to their bedroom. "It's a fun piece, and that's what attracted me to

it. I saw Luca Buvoli's work for the first time a few years ago at the Venice Bienniale and knew I would want to own something of his one day. Fairs are a wonderful way to discover art and artists from all over the world, especially artists who are breaking new ground."

By her own admission, art has changed Fran Ruwitch's life. Because she didn't want to go back in time, her mission is very narrow. She chooses art that has a nervous quality and a provocative presence. She acquired what many consider high-risk art because, Fran says, "I was willing to have my comfort zone pushed." Lee is totally supportive; together they've established an endowment fund for art education at the Lowe Art Museum in Miami. Although Lee is conservative by nature, he explains, "I'm in the high-risk business of real estate and joint ventures, and I can appreciate the excitement Fran finds in her adventurous search for art of the moment."

I COVERED THE WALLS WITH A SPINACH-GREEN MATT FABRIC. THE PAINTINGS NOW SHINE AND GLOW WITH LIFE.

Although it is difficult to imagine a traditional English country house without pictures, until about the middle of the seventeenth century the aristocratic class had very little interest in acquiring art. The long galleries attached to these early houses were designed not as exhibition space but as places to take exercise. They were hung with pictures certainly, but these were almost exclusively family portraits. The faces of the relatives that lined the Elizabethan long galleries at Hardwick and Knole, for instance, were intended to reflect the dignity of the family rather than any particular artistic connoisseurship.

It was not until the seventeenth century that King Charles I and members of his court started to collect art seriously. The earl of Arundel was one of the first educated aristocrats to travel to Italy in the early 1600s. Tirelessly he visited monuments and private galleries and was inspired to purchase works and bring them back to England. His noble friends quickly followed suit, and a hundred years later their country estates had become repositories of some of the great treasures of the world.

In many cases, the new aficionados discovered that their houses were not able to accommodate this sudden influx of large canvases, sculptures, and precious objects, and massive remodeling programs took place—additional floor space, higher ceilings, and bigger windows were all de rigueur. Competition between families was intense. When the duchess of Northumberland was planning a new house in 1760, she gave a checklist to one of her friends visiting a rival's country estate to find out what she was up against. After requesting details about the exterior and the gardens, she wanted to know, "Is there a fine Collection of pictures (landscapes, portraits or historical) . . . is the Furniture rich plain neat mean Elegant Expensive?"

These eighteenth-century country houses were what social historian Mark Girouard calls "power houses"; that is, they served as showcases for their owners, whose choice of architect, designer, and art all combined in establishing the patron's status in the world. Thus how one's paintings and furniture were displayed was of the highest significance. It was now considered advisable to have the works of art placed in the living and dining rooms, informally juxtaposed with equally high quality furniture and furnishings, so that visitors could be entertained for meals or *musicales* directly beneath the works of a Raphael or a Michelangelo.

OPPOSITE

An "enfilade" at Boughton House, with a delicate green wallcovering, a black and white tile floor, and seventeenth-century portraits on the walls.

OVERLEAF

A golden light bathes the library at Boughton in a warm glow. Because the room has such high ceilings, the paintings—all portraits—form an aristocratic line-up above the bookshelves.

This was not always a simple matter, however. J. B. S. Morritt admitted a slight problem with the positioning of his provocative portrait of Velázquez's *Venus with a Mirror,* known as the Rokeby Venus. He finally decided to place it over a high chimneypiece in his library. "It is an admirable light for the painting and shows it to perfection, whilst by raising the said backside to a considerable height the ladies may avert their downcast eyes without difficulty." At Holkham Hall in Norfolk, Lord Leicester had a "landscape room" where paintings by Claude,

In the morning room at Drumlanrig. The portrait over the fireplace is of the Countess of Dalkieth, the present Duchess of Buccleuch, by John Merton (1957). The small engravings on each side of the mantel are notable French personalities of the 1680s. The landscapes of Windsor Castle on the far wall are by Paul Sandby (1725–1809).

Poussin, and Salvator Rosa were hung alongside windows looking out over comparable views of woods and lakes.

The present duke of Buccleuch has three houses, two in Scotland and one in England, which contain art amassed over three hundred years, mostly through strategic marriages with wealthy families in the seventeenth and eighteenth centuries. Like his ancestors, the duke is greatly interested in how the pictures look. At Drumlanrig Castle in Dumfriesshire, he points out, "If you lie on your back underneath the 1670s silver chandelier on the staircase, it must be the only place in the world where you can see simultaneously a Rembrandt, a Holbein, and a Leonardo da Vinci."

The pictures have been arranged with regard to which ancestral branch collected or commissioned them for which house, and also according to their history. "As

*The paintings above the Louis XV writing table in the gallery hall
at Bowhill are* The Countess of Perth *by Sir Anthony Van Dyck on
the left, and on the right,* Mary Villiers, Duchess of Richmond,
by the studio of Sir Anthony Van Dyck.

BELOW

*In the dining room at Bowhill, the little girl in the portrait is of Lady
Caroline Scott by Sir Joshua Reynolds. The story is that she came in
from the snow one day while Reynolds was painting her brother and he
was so enchanted, he painted her, too.*

well as keeping family portraits together," he explains,
"there is the matter of suitable background color
schemes. For instance, in one house a room was painted
post war in pale blue-green. It was a pretty color but
made the paintings look dirty and dingy, so I covered the
walls with a spinach-green matt fabric. The paintings now
shine and glow with life."

225

For families like the Buccleuchs, the art is both a
blessing and a burden. Preserving it, showing it to the
public, protecting it from harm are huge responsibilities.
But the rooms in which these treasures are displayed
exude warmth, timelessness, and above all, the ease and
confidence that comes from having been host to these
rare pictures and objects over many years.

"There are few features of a historic house that
leave a more powerful and lingering impression than
atmosphere," the duke says. "Over hundreds of years it is
hardly surprising that such emotions as happiness or sorrow, love or hatred, should leave their marks, perhaps in
metaphysical terms like color schemes in decor, the style
of paintings and furniture collected, but more usually in a
cocktail of abstract sensations that can only be summa-
rized by the word 'atmosphere.'"

JEAN & JAY KISLAK

WE DIDN'T TRY TO CREATE A MUSEUM. . . . WE WERE DETERMINED TO LIVE COMFORTABLY AND INTIMATELY WITH THE ART WE LOVE.

The Kislaks are great travelers who move as easily back in time as they do across continents. Like their stamp-spattered passports (thirty-five countries) and their library of 14,000 books, the art that distinguishes their high-rise Miami duplex chronicles the journey they've made to bring home a bounty of beauty.

Jay and Jean see their home as a "voyage of discovery," and its assemblage of art from various cultures, countries, and periods as exhilarating and compatible. It encompasses the ancient Egyptian artifacts and modern paintings they began collecting when they first married, the eighteenth-century Romney portraits of Lady Hamilton that Jean identifies with, and the pre-Columbian objects that Jay collects because they complement his library of books on the discovery of Mexico, Florida, and the Caribbean. "Our interests in travel, books, and art all go together—it's a continuum," Jean explains.

From the very beginning, acquiring art has been an adventure for the Kislaks. "We bought our first painting together just before we married," Jean recalls. "It was

OPPOSITE

Miró's Night Cat, Day Cat *prowls the top of the steps, and a Mayan floor sculpture guards the staircase wall that displays a Miró drawing and an Art Deco painting by an unknown artist. A Malaysian calling horn stands before a Lucian Freud oil, and Modigliani and Renoir drawings.*

Richard Diebenkorn's *Berkeley 6*. We found it at a Sotheby's auction in New York and didn't think it would go above the estimated price. But I loved it and just kept bidding and bidding, going way past what Jay and I had planned to spend. Before I knew it, I had set a world record for Diebenkorn's work."

"Our Diebenkorn is the first thing I see when I wake up in the morning," Jay tells you. "It faces our bed. Jean hung it above a 3,000-year-old Egyptian wooden cat. She loves mixing things up and changing things around. She has an eye for it. Somehow it works."

Because the Kislaks travel almost six months of the year, they are sensitive to the importance of creating an environment that is as nurturing and relaxing for them as it is appropriate for the art. Although many of their artworks require a dominance of space, they don't take over the rooms in which the Kislaks live and entertain. "We didn't try to create a museum," Jean says, "or to exalt the purity of a collection. We were determined to live comfortably and intimately with the art we love." Jean chose low lighting and a soothing spectrum of grays, whites, and beiges for the walls and upholstered furniture because, she says, "I thought it would be attractive and not fight with the art." To diffuse the powerful presence of the hundreds of artworks, Jean integrated family photographs, personal objects, and vases filled with flowers on modern glass and antique wood tables. "There is art

The Kislaks' serpentine library integrates paintings, tapestries, and art objects with Jay's formidable collection of art and history books.

around to look at, if you want to, but you don't feel assaulted by it," Jean says.

In the living room Jean has seated two Nayarit Mexican sculptures dating back to A.D. 400 on either side of a lace-covered coffee table. "We named them Ed and Shirley," Jean laughs. "There are some pieces that we enjoy so much they have become personalities."

Jean feels mystically drawn to the notorious eighteenth-century English beauty Emma Hamilton and talks about the three George Romney portraits she has acquired. "A hypnotist regressed me to the eighteenth century, and I learned I may be related to one of Emma's daughters," she says. In addition to Romney's *Sensibility* in the bedroom, she hung his *Portrait of Lady Emma* in her dressing room where "I could be close to it every day." And Jean created a ceremonial setting in the dining area for Romney's *Bacchante,* one of his first portraits of Emma, done when she was eighteen. Beneath the painting, a still life of books, letters, and documents about Emma are arranged in homage to the woman who holds such a presence here. A miniature portrait of Emma is included on the cover of Madame Marie Vigée-Lebrun's book, *Portraits of Great French and English Beauties of the*

228

Eighteenth Century. In startling juxtaposition, a Mayan shaman stands guard, transforming the nineteenth-century English cabinet into an altar for the Emma Hamilton memorabilia.

Jay triggered Jean's fascination with Emma Hamilton six years ago by calling her attention to a letter Emma had written that was up for auction. It was the first of twelve letters and twenty-five books devoted to Emma that Jean collected, adding another dimension to the massive collection of books and documents that Jay began long before they married. His collection includes cherished books, documents, and maps on the early history and discovery of America, notably manuscripts by Hernán Cortés and several letters written by Christopher Columbus. They are conserved in a serpentine library off the living room. "It was architecturally planned so you would wind your way through a labyrinth of books and art," Jean says, leading you to an Edward Curtis photograph, *The Vanishing Race,* a Japanese samurai screen, a Picasso ceramic, and a trove of Chalcolithic oil pots, dating back to thousands of years before Christ, which Jay found in Israel. Paintings, tapestries, and antiquities combine with books to create a room that, Jean says, "has more character than the other rooms in our home." It's one of several quiet zones the Kislaks have created in which to enjoy their books and art.

A witty arrangement of disparate art is on view in the Kislaks' bedroom where Richard Diebenkorn's Berkeley 6 *hangs above a table that displays Jay's new collection of pocket globes, a 3,000-year-old Egyptian wooden cat, a Picasso bird, and a Japanese sword. Looking on is a Mayan bust they call* Buster.

An Indonesian temple bird sanctifies the master bedroom. Plaster panels that once belonged to Madame Du Barry are an extension of the headboard. Filtering light from the window is an artist-carved screen brought back from Moscow.

Buster *also watches over Jean's favorite painting,* Sensibility, *Romney's eighteenth-century portrait of Lady Hamilton.*

I OFTEN ADMIRE ART I WOULD NOT WANT IN MY LIVING ROOM.

One can almost hear the lush strains of George Gershwin's *An American in Paris* as one enters this floating world above the river Seine. The American in this case is Bertrand Taylor, who, with his wife, Fay, owns a Paris pied-à–terre whose rooms offer a powerful visual confirmation of his declaration, "I'm at home abroad." With a spectacular view of Notre-Dame and the Île Saint-Louis from the balcony, the apartment is itself a work of art, in particular the salon, where colorist paintings, pink and green jade, Oriental carpets and fabrics, and family heirlooms all combine in an endless perspective of mirrored magic.

The apartment sits directly beneath the famous restaurant Le Tour d'Argent; a private staircase connects them. Bert Taylor's father lived here, having moved to Paris in 1949 after serving in the Second World War. On his death in 1972, his son took possession of it, along with his father's collection of furniture, decorative objects, carpets, and pictures—and his racing stable.

Bert kept the the horses until 1979. He also kept a lot of his father's furniture and furnishings. "My parents always lived in lovely places," he recalls. "But I was the one who really pursued a certain *design*. I was always interested in how you put everything together."

Bert was the one, for instance, who decided to mirror the walls and ceiling of the salon. "Paris is a study in tonalities of grays," he observes. "I love those colors. I also love water and anything made of glass. The mirrors enhance all these passions of mine." The rest of the apartment is less theatrical but equally elegant: there are two bedrooms along a narrow corridor, which contains the Taylors' "rogue's gallery" of photographs, with a kitchen at the end.

231

OPPOSITE

The piercing blues in Carré's painting, with its delicately molded silver frame (which was very hard to find), make the mirrors gleam more brightly. In their reflection, Bertrand Taylor.

ABOVE

From Bertrand Taylor's silvery living room one looks out to the glories of Notre Dame and the skies of Paris, the City of Light.

The art takes its place, without calling attention to itself, as part of the ensemble Bert has carefully put together. The Chinese Sung blue paintwork in the salon, for instance, has the same value, in Bert's eyes, as the moldings, the carpet, the jade in the vitrines, and the paintings. No single element is promoted over another, but each is integrated into the overall look that the owner wishes to achieve. Some art lovers regard the decoration

The bedroom has a whole wall consisting of one work of art—an eighteenth-century Chinese silk paneled screen. It was converted into a wall installation while retaining the original wooden frames.

of their living space as secondary to their art; others, like Bert Taylor, see art as a bit player in the larger drama, in which colors, furniture, and other features of a room play just as vital a role.

"Some people buy art because it's significant," he says. "But I often admire art I would not want in my living room. For example, a Vlaminck that my father owned used to hang in the salon. But the painting was too angry in feeling and too muddy in color for my taste." Bert sold the Vlaminck in favor of a much lesser known French artist, Carré, whose work he fell in love with in a Paris

gallery. "I walked by and kept going back," he said. "The colors, vitality, and skill in portraying water and boats delight me."

Other family works of art passed the son's test. A charming oil by Ludwig Bemelmans, a friend of Bert's father, illustrating one of the Madeline stories, hangs in the corridor. Nearby is a series of photographs of the Villa Madama in Rome, restored in the 1920s by Bert's sister, Dorothy, and her husband, Prince Carlo di Frasso. A shimmering eighteenth-century Chinese silk paneled screen belonging to his father has been cunningly affixed, still in its wood frames, to the walls of the master bedroom. He has added to his father's Chinese jade collection over the years, along with other glass and porcelain decorative objects.

Bert and Fay, an amateur painter, travel regularly between four places in the United States and France, each with its own character, each of which they call home. "I believe life is a stage set," he says. "You move from one scene to another. The Japanese understand this. Our living spaces are like way stations on our journey through life. For me, some elements are constant: color, light, water. Here in the Paris apartment, they come together in a way that's very satisfying."

LEFT

In the hall, a rich combination of colors is produced by two Tunisian glass paintings—a favorite genre of Bert's—and a Chinese lacquer tea chest inherited from his father. The red damask wall covering highlights the exotic artworks.

BELOW

In a mirrored vitrine in the salon, a French lithograph by Cathelin is inscribed to Bert's father and stepmother. His father's large collection of jade, added to by Bert, reflects both men's fascination with Oriental works of art.

OVERLEAF

The reflecting salon is like a jewelbox, with the colors of the Chinese rug playing a subtle role. On the right hangs a twentieth-century work by the French artist Carré. Opposite is a portrait of Bert Taylor's stepmother by James King, known as Vinciates.

WE LUST FOR WALLS. WE DON'T PUSH ART UNDER THE BEDS OR PUT IT AWAY IN CLOSETS.

They describe themselves as two fiercely independent people held together by an all-consuming love of art. "It was the only thing that kept the marriage going for nearly fifty years," Ruth says laughingly, "since we worked in such different worlds."

Formerly a county commissioner and a nominee for mayor of Miami, Ruth is now president of the Dade Community Foundation that, among many things, supports the arts. In addition to heading up his own entertainment production company, Richard has worked with several regional museums and the Whitney Museum on their print acquisition programs.

The Shacks have been acquiring art ever since they decided that their future was in Miami. "We came here on our honeymoon in 1953 and never left," Richard says. "At the time we had no money but decided that for birthdays or anniversaries, we would give each other a gift of art, but it had to be under a hundred dollars."

The only things they could afford then were the

prints Tatyana Grosman was doing at Universal Limited Art Editions. Ruth remembers going to her Long Island studio and watching the works being done. "It was transforming," she says. "We ended up with Jasper Johns' flags and targets, prints by Helen Frankenthaler, Larry Rivers, and Jim Dine as well as Richard's favorite piece, Rauschenberg's *Stuntman 1, 2, and 3.*"

Because the Shacks occupy an entire floor with a 360-degree view of Miami, they've created sunrise and sunset rooms, filling each with art that is appropriate in mood and spirit. Ruth tells you, "When I wake up, I like to walk into our morning room, where we've hung Rauschenberg's *Sling Shot,* and see the sun filling it with oranges, reds, and blues. At the end of the day, we retreat to our living room to watch the sun go down. It's a tranquil room that's rich in meaning for us since it contains my mother's needlepoint chairs and the vibrant works of Latin American and Florida artists we found early on."

Describing the challenge of finding the right place in their home for each of the 450 artworks they've acquired, Ruth remarks, "We lust for walls. We don't push art under the beds or put it away in closets. It's important for us to see the art we love every day and remember how we felt when we first saw it."

OPPOSITE

The Shacks stacked two discordant paintings one on top of the other. Willi Moser's Am Ruden Platz *and Roy Lichtenstein's* Blue Floor Interior *yet work together to create an astonishing viewing room that looks out on Biscayne Bay. Sculptures by Ingrid Hartlieb (center) and Sebastian Trovato (corner) add gravity to the room.*

Richard and Ruth sit on pillows beneath a Robert Petersen acrylic on canvas with collage in their sun-filled morning room.

Because the gallery library has limited light, Richard chose it to exhibit his photography collection. Timothy Greenfield-Sanders' portraits of New York artists are positioned at eye level on a molding for easy viewing and arranging. Lichtenstein's painting of a mirrored interior is reflected in the mirrored wall.

The Shacks filled their morning room with edgy works of art, including (from left to right) Rauschenberg's Sling Shot 4, *two Larry Rivers prints, a Cesar Trasobares assemblage, and a mixed media piece by Pietro Finelli. The shelves filled with quirky objects create an amusing alcove topped by Richard Hamilton's namesake sign.*

IN THE SPOTLIGHT

HOW TO LIGHT ART

Interior lighting schemes are always a challenge, whether you are a professional decorator or an amateur. But while you may hesitate about where in a room to place floor or table lamps, it is clear that if you have pictures and sculptures, they become your first priority. Indeed when you have decided how to light your art, you may have solved the problem of how to light your rooms.

Before electricity, there were a limited number of ways to illuminate art: daylight, candlelight, and oil and gas lamps. The use of heavy gilded frames for almost all framing prior to the twentieth century was partly due to the fact that the gold reflected the candlelight and enhanced the impact of the pictures. Today we have many more choices, and much more information to digest before making our lighting decisions.

Most consultants agree that natural light is the best light for pictures. The nineteenth-century British art collector and architectural designer Sir John Soane revolutionized museum lighting in his 1811 design for the Dulwich Picture Gallery, just outside London. He insisted on a single-story building with every room lit by the soft glow of skylights.

But—and it is a big "but"—natural light has to be distinguished from sunlight. Direct sunlight must not fall on wood, cloth, paper, oils, and other fugitive mediums. From a conservator's point of view, the first rule of lighting art is to avoid the ultraviolet rays from the sun, which can irreversibly damage or fade the artwork. All light fades art over time, but UV, invisible to the human eye, is the most damaging.

Remember, too, that while exterior daylight may measure 10,000 foot-candles, you should not allow more than 5 to 40 foot-candles to reach your art, depending on the medium, watercolors and works on paper being the most vulnerable. This may mean installing special blinds or screens over your windows to filter out the sun. Someone building a new house has the opportunity to specify windows with specially treated Plexiglas or a UV film to protect pictures and furniture. For the rest of us, meshlike scrims or blinds to counteract overbright daylight are now readily available in stores specializing in window treatments.

After dark, of course, alternative lighting must be used. Electric light for art comes in various forms, most commonly from track lighting, recessed ceiling lights, or table or floor lamps. The old-fashioned method of attaching a picture light to the frame with a tubular bulb hanging over the painting does provide evenly spread light but is customarily more often used with traditional works than with modern art. Track lighting and recessed

A wall installation by Donald Lipski in Ann Hatch's San Francisco house is unified by a series of recessed halogen spotlights that project arcs of light over the art.

Responding to the challenge of lighting Lynda Benglis's wall sculpture and an African fetish piece, Jane and Gerald Katcher installed long cone-shaped sconces on each side of the mantel in their Florida living room.

ceiling lights project a very focused point of light on pictures and sculptures. Portable can-lights situated on the floor or on any flat surface also project light directly at the artworks for a dramatic effect. Halogen bulbs, with their extraordinary brilliance, have recently become very popular. To see the effect of these, visit the Frick Collection in New York, much of which has recently been relit with customized halogen over-frame spotlights, giving a very intense illumination to the paintings. Halogen track lighting is popular with interior designers and homeowners, because the light is highly concentrated and the fixtures are smaller than regular track installations. However, problems may arise with this intense light source. According to Charles G. Stone II, partner in Fisher Marantz Renfro Stone, a firm which for over thirty years has provided lighting advice to museums, residences, theaters, and public spaces, "Very small light sources can cause sharp shadows and glare. The addition of spread lenses and louvers can partially overcome the problem."

Table and floor lamps offer a more diffuse light, with far less intensity and brightness. Light from shaded lamps rarely falls directly on the picture the way track lighting does, and often paintings benefit from this softer illumination. The warm glow from a table lamp with an incan-

descent bulb can make an old master painting, for instance, seem particularly rich in color and depth. A lampshade made of glass or silk may provide additional light for art. Other sources, most notably fluorescent, are also used, but these are less common in private homes because of the large size of the fittings and the expense of dimming.

From a conservation point of view, electric light is not so problematic as sunlight, but the heat from lightbulbs—in particular, halogen bulbs—can damage pictures. Moreover, no artificial light is as accurate from the color-spectrum point of view as natural daylight. But when we see a Tiepolo glowing in the candlelight of an Italian church, we are not likely to care about that.

Lighting Considerations

1. Where should the light *live*? This is a question about aesthetics, not hardware. "Try to define the task of your lighting scheme," Charles Stone suggests. "Do you want a soft overall glow in your room or a point source focusing on individual objects? Or do you want both?"

2. Are you lighting paintings or sculpture? Obviously the lighting of a Giacometti in a hallway requires different lighting than a watercolor in the study.

3. Consider whether your art will be viewed from a distance or close up. Lighting should be adjusted taking into account the proximity of the viewer.

4. How large is each piece of art? A very big canvas requires more diffuse light than a miniature.

5. Where was the picture painted? An eighteenth-century English landscape, for instance, was probably painted in a cool north light and should not be lit from an intensely bright electric source.

6. Visit museums and galleries. If the lighting they use pleases you, perhaps you can adapt their techniques for use with your own works of art.

CARE AND CONSERVATION AIDS

The American Institute for Conservation of Historic and Artistic Works
1717 K Street NW, Suite 301
Washington, D.C. 20006
(202) 452-9545
Fax (202) 452-9328
E-mail: InfoAIC@aol.com

The AIC is a national membership organization of conservation professionals dedicated to preserving the art and historic artifacts of our cultural heritage for future generations. The ÅIC publishes brochures on every aspect of art collecting and conservation and will mail them to you free of charge.

Its nonprofit Foundation of the American Institute for Conservation of Historic and Artistic Works (same address as above) offers educational programs, grants to conservators, and a *free* referral system. To find a conservator in your area, the AIC national office can provide the local information you require. In response to your inquiry, a computer-generated list of conservators is compiled and grouped by location, specialization, type of service provided, and AIC membership category.

The AIC brochure *Guidelines for Selecting a Conservator* can help you decide whether you need one, and how to go about making your decision.

Museums may also offer guidance on conservation. For a museum closest to your area, write:

American Association of Museums
1225 Eye Street NW
Washington, D.C. 20005

The Museums & Galleries Commission
16 Queen Anne's Gate
London SW1H 9AA, England

PUBLICATIONS

Caring for Your Collections: Preserving and Protecting Your Art and Other Collectibles
National Committee to Save America's Cultural Collections
Harry M. Abrams, Inc.
100 Fifth Avenue
New York, NY 10011

Curatorial Care of Works of Art on Paper: Basic Procedures for Paper Preservation
Ann Clapp
Lyons and Burford
31 West 21st Street
New York, NY 10010

Caring for Collections: Strategies for Conservation, Maintenance and Documentation
American Association of Museums
Department 4002
Washington, D.C. 20042-4002

The Art of the Conservator
Edited by Andrew Oddy
Smithsonian Institution Press
Department 900
Blue Ridge Summit, PA 17294

Conservation Concerns: A Guide for Collectors and Curators
Edited by Konstanze Bachman
Smithsonian Institution Press
Department 900
Blue Ridge Summit, PA 17294

The prints and drawings center in the National Gallery is home to the Vogel Collection. The staff has curated and cataloged 90,000 works on paper, protected in custom-made cabinets and made available to the public by appointment. On easels and tables are works by LeWitt, the Mangolds, Christo, Tuttle, Renouf, and a portrait by Will Barnet.

*Journal of the American Institute
for Conservation*
The American Institute for
Conservation of Historic and
Artistic Works
1400 16th Street NW
Suite 340
Washington, D.C. 20036

*Guide to Environmental Protection
of Collections*
Barbara Appelbaum
Sound View Press
170 Post Road
Madison, CT 06443

The Care of Prints and Drawings
Margaret E. Ellis
Altamira Press
2455 Teller Road
Thousand Oaks, CA 91320

*Life of a Photograph: Archival Processing,
Matting, Framing and Storage*
Dennis Inch and Laurance Keefe
Focal Press
225 Wildwood Avenue
Woburn, MA 01801

The Care of Photographs
Siegfried Rempel
Nick Lyons Books
31 West 21st Street
New York, NY 10010

The Textile Conservator's Manual
Sheila Landi
Butterworth and Heinemann
225 Wildwood Avenue
Woburn, MA 01801

A fuller listing is available from the
American Institute for Conservation of
Historic and Artistic Works, see above.

Several art magazines have published
issues with encyclopedic listings of
sources, including:

Art & Auction
P.O. Box 37502
Boone, IA 50037-0052
(800) 777-8718
The magazine's "International Directory" includes auction houses, galleries, museums, fairs, and art services
such as restoration and conservation,
framing, shipping and storing, and
insurance.

*This nineteenth-century American portrait is
one of many in Ralph Esmerian's folk art
collection.*

Art in America
P.O. Box 37003
Boone, IA 50037-0003
(800) 925-8059
The magazine's "Sourcebook to the
U.S. Art World" lists galleries, dealers,
museums, artists, art catalogs and arti-
cles, art services, and art schools.

COLLECTING

*The Best of Everything: An Insider's
Guide to Collecting—for Every Taste and
Every Budget.*
John L. Marion and Christopher
Andersen
Simon & Schuster
1230 Avenue of the Americas
New York, NY 10020

BUYING ART

Before you buy a work of art, it is
worth checking on its provenance,
particularly today when many pictures
up for sale or auction seem to have
some unresolved ownership issue. The
following organization may help you:

**International Foundation for Art
Research**
500 Fifth Avenue
Suite 1234
New York, NY 10110
(212) 391-6234
Fax (212) 391-8794

The following two database companies
can screen artworks for a prospective
buyer:

Art Loss Register
666 Fifth Avenue
21st Floor
New York, NY 10103
(212) 262-4831
Fax (212) 262-4838
www.artloss.com

Trans-Art
200 L Street NW
Washington, D.C. 20036
(202) 737-4913
Fax (202) 628-0627

SELLING ART

The first step is to get the work
appraised. Auction houses and dealers
will appraise, but they may not offer a
completely objective appraisal. Three
independent sources may be consulted:

The American Society of Appraisers
555 Herndon Parkway
Suite 125
Herndon, VA 20170
(800) 272-8258

**The Appraisers Association
of America**
386 Park Avenue South
Suite 2000
New York, NY 10016
(212) 889-5404
Fax (212) 889-5503

International Society of Appraisers
Riverview Plaza Office Park
16040 Christensen Road, Suite 320
Seattle, WA 98188
(206) 241-0359
Fax (206) 241-0436
www.isa-appraisers.org

A wonderful painting by William Hawkins exemplifies the quality of John and Margaret Robson's collection of outsider art.

To sell, auction houses or dealers are the best bet. They will advise you on setting a fair price. Auction houses generally charge 15 percent of the first $50,000 and 10 percent above that, but also add other fees. Dealers charge less (usually 20 percent of the selling price) and can often act faster than auction houses, which may not immediately be able to schedule a sale in which your artwork will be appropriate.

The major auction houses are:

Butterfield & Butterfield
220 San Bruno Avenue
San Francisco, CA 94103
(415) 861-7500
Fax (415) 861-8951
or
7601 Sunset Boulevard
Los Angeles, CA 90046
(213) 850-7500
Fax (213) 850-5843
(with offices in Sydney, Vienna, Paris, and London)

Christie's
502 Park Avenue
New York, NY 10022
(212) 546-1000
Fax (212) 752-3956
www.christies.com
(with offices in North and South America, Europe, and Asia)

William Doyle Galleries
175 East 87th Street
New York, NY 10128
(212) 427-2730
Fax (212) 369-0892
(with offices in Washington, DC, and Florida)

Sloan's Auction Galleries
4920 Wyaconda Road
North Bethesda, MD 20852
(301) 468-4911
Fax (301) 468-9182

Sotheby's
1334 York Avenue
New York NY 10021
(212) 606-7000
Fax (212) 606-7022
www.sothebys.com
(with offices in 46 countries throughout the world)

For dealers, consult:

The Art Dealers Association of America
575 Madison Avenue
New York, NY 10022
(212) 940-8590
Fax (212) 940-7013
www.artdealers.org

The Society of Fine Art Auctioneers
7 Blenheim Street
London W1, England
(171) 233-4200

SHIPPING AND TRANSPORTATION

The following organizations will help you store and/or ship your artworks both nationally and internationally:

Masterpiece International Ltd.
New York area:
(212) 825-7000
Fax (212) 825-7010

Washington, DC, area:
(703) 661-6881
Fax (703) 661-6885

Chicago area:
(847) 806-9595
Fax: (847) 806-9599

Los Angeles area:
(310) 215-9861
Fax: (310) 215-9862

Fine Arts Express Worldwide
Head office, Boston:
(617) 566-1155
Fax (617) 566-1621

Los Angeles Packing and Crating
(213) 937-2669
Fax (213) 566-1621

Lebron Brothers
New York
(718) 274-0532

Terry Dowd
Chicago
(773) 342-8686
Fax (773) 342-8650

The following publication might be helpful:

Art in Transit: Handbook for Packing and Transporting Paintings
Edited by Mervin Richard, Marion F. Mecklenburg, and Toss M. Merrill
National Gallery of Art
Washington, DC

LIGHTING

To find a lighting designer in your area, write to:

International Association of Lighting Designers
18 East 16th Street
New York, NY 10003
(212) 206-1281

The following manufacturers sell products that illuminate artworks:

Edison Price
409 East 60th Street
New York, NY 10022
(212) 838-5212

Lighting Services Inc. (LSI)
Industrial Park, Route 9W
Stony Point, NY 10980
(914) 942-2800

STAFF Lighting
300 Route 9W
Highland Park, NY 12528
(914) 691-6262

LIGHTOLIER
100 Lighting Way
Secaucus, NJ 07094
(201) 864-3000
*Sales offices throughout the United States
and Canada.*

FRAMING

Publications:

*Decor—The Business Magazine of Fine
Art and Framing*
Commerce Publishing Co.
330 North Fourth Street
St. Louis, Missouri 63102
(314) 421-5445
Fax (314) 421-1070

The Art of Framing
Piers and Caroline Feetham
Clarkson Potter/Publishers
201 East 50th Street
New York, NY 10022

Selected Framers:

Artifact
1650 20th Street
Santa Monica, CA 90404
(310) 315-2144

Bark Frameworks
85 Grand Street
New York, NY 10013
(212) 431-9080

English Gallery
6 Old Street Road
Peterborough, NH 03458
(603) 924-9044

Frameway Studio
875 North Orleans Street
Chicago, IL 60610
(312) 751-1660

Gerlach Frames
240 Bedford Avenue
Brooklyn, NY 11211
(718) 486-8836

Guttmann Picture Frame Associates
180 East 73rd Street
New York, NY 10021
(212) 744-8600

Hobbs & Tolley Studios
734 15th Street NW
Washington, DC 20005
(202) 347-0003

Richard Tobey Fine Frames
741 North La Cienega Boulevard
Los Angeles, CA 90069
(310) 652-8023 or (800) 831-7128

GREAT PRIVATE HOUSE COLLECTIONS OPEN TO THE PUBLIC

UNITED STATES

The Barnes Foundation
300 North Latches Lane
Merion, PA 19066
(610) 667-0290

The Frick Collection
1 East 70th Street
New York, NY 10021
(212) 288-0700

Isabella Stewart Gardner Museum
280 The Fenway
Boston, MA 02115
(617) 566-1401

The Huntington Library
1151 Oxford Road
San Marino, CA 91108
(626) 405-2140

The Pierpont Morgan Library
29 East 36th Street
New York, NY 10016
(212) 685-0610

Olana
RD 2
Hudson, NY 12534
(518) 828-1035

The Phillips Collection
1600 21st Street NW
Washington, DC 20009
(202) 387-2151

EUROPE

Waddesdon Manor
Waddesdon
Nr. Aylesbury HP18 0JH, England
01296-651226

Hatchlands Park
East Clandon
Guildford GU4 7RT, England
01483-222482
Infoline 01483-223479

Sir John Soane's Museum
13 Lincoln's Inn Fields
London, England
171-405-2107

The Wallace Collection
Hertford House
Manchester Square
London W1, England
l71-935-0687

Musée Jacquemart-André
158 Boulevard Haussmann
Paris 75008, France
1-01.42.89.04.91

*The Fools by Arturo Rodriguez from
Ramón and Nercys Cernuda's Cuban art
collection.*

Midnight, Big Raggedy Ann *(1992–3)* by Jennifer Bartlett hangs in the library of the artist's New York home.

Musée Nissim de Camondo
63 Rue de Monceau
Paris 75008, France
1-01.53.89.06.40

The Peggy Guggenheim Collection
Palazzo Venier dei Leoni
Dorsoduro 701
30123 Venice, Italy
41-706-288

ART IN CYBERSPACE

For art news on the web:
www.artdaily.com

On-line art information services offer searches on artists, prices, subject matter, provenance, dealers, and auction house news and schedules. See listings above for some art-related sites. Others include:

ArtNet Worldwide
145 East 75th Street
New York, NY 10022
(212) 497-9700
Fax (212) 497-9707
www.artnet.com

Art Systems for Collectors
(212) 741-1906
Fax (212) 741-1846
www.artsystems.com

The Interoffice Collector
www.icollector.com

Most art museums both in the United States and Europe are now on-line and have Web sites providing all kinds of information on art and artists. Here are some of the largest:

UNITED STATES

Art Institute of Chicago
Chicago, Illinois
www.artic.edu

Brooklyn Museum of Art
Brooklyn, New York
www.brooklynart.org

Dallas Museum of Art
Dallas, Texas
www.dm-art.org

J. Paul Getty Museum
Malibu, California
www.getty.edu/museum

Solomon R. Guggenheim Museum
New York, New York
www.guggenheim.org

The Jewish Museum
New York, New York
www.thejewishmuseum.org

Los Angeles County Museum of Art
Los Angeles, California
www.lacma.org

The Metropolitan Museum of Art
New York, New York
www.metmuseum.org

Museum of Fine Arts
Boston, Massachusetts
www.mfa.org

Museum of Modern Art
New York, New York
www.moma.org

National Gallery of Art
Washington, DC
www.nga.gov

Philadelphia Museum of Art
Philadelphia, Pennsylvania
www.philamuseum.org

San Francisco Museum of Modern Art
San Francisco, California
www.sfmoma.org

Walker Art Center
Minneapolis, Minnesota
www.walker.org

Whitney Museum of American Art
New York, New York
www.echonyc.com/~whitney

EUROPE

The British Museum
London
www.british-museum.ac.uk

The National Gallery
London
www.nationalgallery.org.uk

The National Portrait Gallery
London
www.npg.org.uk

The Tate Gallery
London
www.tate.org.uk

The Louvre
Paris
mistral.culture.fr/louvre

Alte Pinakothek
Munich
www.stmukwk.bayerr.de/kunst/museen

Uffizi Galleries
Florence
www.uffizi.firenze.it

The Vatican Museums
Rome
www.christusrex.org

Museo del Prado
Madrid
http:/museoprado.mcu.es

PERMISSIONS

Poems

6: "One Vision" by Susan Baran. Copyright © 1999 by Susan Baran.
46: "Digression on *Number 1, 1948*" from Frank O'Hara. Copyright © 1971 by Maureen Granville-Smith, Administratix of the Estate of Frank O'Hara. Reprinted by permission of Alfred A. Knopf Inc.
116: Excerpts from *Self-Portrait in a Convex Mirror* by John Ashbery. Copyright © 1972, 1973, 1974, 1975 by John Ashbery. Used by permission of Viking Penguin, a division of Penguin Putnam Inc.
166: "A Study of Two Pears" from *Collected Poems* by Wallace Stevens. Copyright © 1942 by Wallace Stevens and renewed 1970 by Holly Stevens. Reprinted by permission of Alfred A. Knopf Inc.
200: "Poem in Which a Painting Becomes a Poem" by John Yau. Copyright © 1999 by John Yau.

Art

Cover: *Flower Silkscreen* by Andy Warhol. Copyright © 1999 Andy Warhol Foundation for the Visual Arts/ARS, New York. Also reproduced in the interior of the book.
Cover: *Hagmatana 1 Protractor Series* (1967) by Frank Stella. Copyright © 1999 Frank Stella/Artists Rights Society (ARS), New York. Also reproduced in the interior of the book.
Chapter dividers: Details from: **6-7:** *The Red Sea* (1995), **46-47:** *Weather* (1995), **84-85:** *The Two of Them* (1988–90), **116-117:** *Inheritance-7* (1998), **166-167:** *In the Temple* (1989–90), **200-201:** *Oracle* (1992–3) by Max Gimblett. Used by permission.
Half-title page: *Cross Aweigh* (1967) by Alfonso Ossorio. Copyright © 1999 by the Ossorio Foundation/Michael Rosenfeld Galley.
19: *Portrait of the Gierloffs* by Edvard Munch. Copyright © 1999 by the Munch Museum/The Munch-Ellingson Group/Artists Rights Society (ARS), New York.
49: *Violon d'Ingres* (1924) and Rayographs. Copyright © 1999 by Man Ray Trust/Artists Rights Society (ARS), New York/ADAGP.
50-51: *View* (1983) by Gilbert and George. Used by permission of the artists.
61: *Workers Waving Goodbye* (1991) by Ed McGowin. Used by permission of the artist.
81: *Package* by Christo. The Dorothy and Herbert Vogel Collection, Ailsa Mellon Bruce Fund, Patron's Permanent Fund and Gift of Dorothy and Herbert Vogel, © 1999 Board of Trustees, National Gallery of Art, Washington, 1974, tarpaulin, rope, and wood, .609 x .495 x .381 (24 x 19 1/2 x 15).
82: *Studio Corner in the Morning with Window Light Across the Floor* (1972) by Sylvia Plimack Mangold. Used by permission of the artist.
82: *Wall Drawing No. 681 C* by Sol LeWitt. The Dorothy and Herbert Vogel Collection, Gift of Dorothy Vogel and Herbert Vogel, Trustees, © 1999 Board of Trustees, National Gallery of Art, Washington, 1993, color ink washes.
82: *Red/Green X Within X* by Robert Mangold. The Dorothy and Herbert Vogel Collection, Ailsa Mellon Bruce Fund, Patron's Permanent Fund and Gift of Dorothy and Herbert Vogel, © 1999 Board of Trustees, National Gallery of Art, Washington, 1981, acrylic and graphite on wove paper mounted on paperboard, 1.120 x 1.115 (44 1/8 x 43 7/8).
83: *Primal Energy III (Earth Sounds)* (1989); acrylic on linen, by Edda Renouf. Used by permission of the artist.
83: *Monkey's Recovery for a Darkened Room (Bluebird)* by Richard Tuttle. The Dorothy and Herbert Vogel Collection, Promised Gift of Dorothy Vogel and Herbert Vogel, on loan to the National Gallery of Art, Washington, 1983, wood, wire, acrylic, matboard, string and cloth, 1.016 x .521 x .318 (40 x 20 1/2 x 12 1/2).
92-98: All artworks by Jennifer Bartlett visible in pictures of her home used courtesy of the artist.
104: Wall paintings by Le Corbusier in the Nivola home used by permission of Ruth Nivola.
112: Ektachrome of the Fragonard Room in the Frick Collection, Copyright © The Frick Collection, New York. Photograph by John Bigelow Taylor.
114: Photograph of Olana dining room used by permission of Kurt A. Dolnier. Copyright © by Kurt A. Dolnier.
114: Photograph of Sir John Soane's Museum, London, Copyright © 1995 by Martin Charles. Reproduced by permission of the Trustees of Sir John Soane's Museum.
115: Photograph from the Wallace Collection by Fritz von der Schulenburg. Copyright © Fritz von der Schulenburg/The Interior Archive.
120: *Robe Series, Sepulchre* by Dorothea Rockburne. Copyright © 1976, 1999 by Dorothea Rockburne/ Artists Rights Society (ARS), New York. Used by permission of the artist and ARS.
133: *The Fools* by Arturo Rodriguez. Used by permission of the artist. Also reproduced on page 245.
134: *Bandolero Criollo* by Carlos Enríquez. Used by permission.
136: Painting by John Walker. Used by permission of the artist.
145: *Portrait of Sondra Gilman* by Andy Warhol. Copyright © 1999 Andy Warhol Foundation for the Visual Arts/ARS, New York.
146: Campbell's Soup picture (1985) by Andy Warhol. Copyright © 1999 Andy Warhol Foundation for the Visual Arts/ARS, New York. Campbell's Soup™ licensed by Campbell's Soup Co. All rights reserved/ARS, New York.
178: *Cheers, A Scene from a Mexican Novel* by Susan Daykin. Used by permission of the artist.
215: Paintings by Sean Scully. Copyright © Sean Scully. Used by permission.
216: *Rotate in Void* (1984) by Donald Baechler, copyright © by Donald Baechler. Used by permission.
217: *Old Doje New Bell* (1993) by Stephen Mueller, copyright © by Stephen Mueller. Used by permission.
238: *Color Study 5* by Robert Petersen. Used by permission of the artist.
247: Quote by H. W. Janson, from *History of Art* by H. W. Janson, published by Harry N. Abrams, Inc. All rights reserved.

ART HAS THE POWER
TO PENETRATE TO THE CORE
OF MAN'S BEING.
THE MORE WE KNOW ABOUT
LIFE, THE MORE
WE KNOW ABOUT ART; AND
IN TURN, THE MORE
WE UNDERSTAND ART,
THE MORE WE UNDERSTAND
WHAT IT MEANS TO BE A
HUMAN BEING IN THE
FULLEST SENSE OF THE TERM.

—H. W. JANSON

INDEX